<u>moviesforbusiness.com</u>™

presents

MOVIES FOR LEADERS

Management Lessons from Four All-Time Great Films

Hoosiers
The Wizard of Oz
The Bridge on the River Kwai
Moby Dick

A *Management Goes to the Movies*™ Guide

by

SHAUN O'L. HIGGINS and **COLLEEN STRIEGEL**

New Media Ventures, Inc.

*MOVIES FOR LEADERS: MANAGEMENT LESSONS
FROM FOUR ALL-TIME GREAT FILMS*

ISBN 0–923910–17–4

Shaun O'L. Higgins and Colleen Striegel

A *Management Goes to the Movies*™ Guide
From **moviesforbusiness.com**™ and New Media Ventures, Inc.

RENT THE MOVIES!

Movies in this book are available for sale or rent
from online services and video outlets.

Production Coordinator: Laura B. Lee

Typography and Design: Integrated Composition Systems
and The Oxalis Group

Management Goes to the Movies, **moviesforbusiness.com**, MGTTM
and the New Media Ventures logotype are registered trademarks
of New Media Ventures, Inc.

<u>DON'T MISS</u> THESE OTHER GREAT
MANAGEMENT GOES TO THE MOVIES(TM)
STUDY GUIDES

MOVIES FOR BUSINESS:
Big Screen Lessons in Corporate Vision,
Entrepreneurship, Logistics and Ethics

MOVIES FOR MARKETERS:
Big-Screen Lessons to Help You Find and Sell the Big Idea

MOVIES FOR CEOs:
Big-Screen Lessons in Mergers, Acquisitions, Startups
Restructuring and Succession

AVAILABLE OR FORTHCOMING FROM
<u>moviesforbusiness.com</u>(TM)
and
NEW MEDIA VENTURES, INC.

"<u>REEL</u> BUSINESS LESSONS
FOR <u>REAL</u> BUSINESS PERFORMANCE"

MOVIES FOR LEADERS:

*Management Lessons from Four
All-Time Great Films*

ACKNOWLEDGMENTS

Movies for Leaders is based in large part on comments received from many managers who have participated in the *Management Goes to the Movies*™ program during the past decade. Most of these have been the employees at various Cowles Publishing Company subsidiaries, including *The* (Spokane, Washington) *Spokesman-Review,* New Media Ventures, Inc., and Print Marketing Concepts. Their insights and enthusiasm for the lessons to be learned from films has been the motivating force behind production of the book. Particular thanks goes to W. Stacey Cowles and Elizabeth A. Cowles for enabling publication of the *Management Goes to the Movies*™ guides and creation of the website **moviesforbusiness.com**™.

We are grateful to many colleagues who have suggested films for inclusion in this and other volumes in the MGTTM series. They include James Lessersohn of the New York Times Company; Art Bassin of TV Data, Inc.; Robin Good of Print Marketing Concepts, Inc.; Michael Snell of The Snell Literary Agency; and John Sturm of the Newspaper Association of America.

John Emery, chief archivist for the Auburn-Cord-

Duesenberg Museum in Auburn, Indiana; Graham-Paige expert Ken Dunsire of Fort Wayne, Indiana; the National Museum of Whaling in New Bedford, Massachusetts; and Price/Costco corporation helped us with research. Applied Segmentation Technologies gave us a forum in which to test lessons in the chapter on *Moby Dick.*

A very special thanks goes to Ann Glendening and Laura Lee, each of whom read over preliminary drafts of the manuscript, contributing key thoughts on both the form and substance of each section of the guide. Ms. Lee also prepared the final manuscript for publication and supervised the guide's production.

Finally, we want to recognize the extraordinary contributions of the producers, directors, screenwriters, actors and crews whose collective efforts gave the world the outstanding films on which *Movies for Leaders* and other MGTTM guides are based. It is our fondest hope that the guides will introduce new audiences to their work and provide yet another perspective for appreciating it.

Shaun O'L. Higgins
Colleen Striegel
October 1999

GENERAL INTRODUCTION:

*Why and How to Use Movies
to Build Your Business and Management Skills*

Management Goes to the Movies™ guides are based on experience. For more than a decade, the authors have used movies to train new managers in basic management techniques and theory. We have also used movies to enrich discussions of leading management issues like succession, strategic planning, product development and the creation of mission statements. In all cases, our use of movies has followed four simple steps:

1. Find a movie that is broadly relevant to the training need or issue.
2. Rent or buy copies of the movie for the employees involved and assign them for home viewing.
3. Meet with the person or group after they've seen the movie and discuss the key topics.
4. Take the lessons learned from the movie and discuss how they might be applied (or in some cases, NOT applied) in the workplace.

Sometimes we've sent a package of microwave popcorn and a six-pack of soft drinks home with the managers. If the movie is appropriate for family viewing, we've suggested that spouses and kids join in watching and discussing the film. The results often have been astonishing. For example:

- There's a scene in the Tom Hanks-Jackie Gleason film *Nothing in Common* in which an ad agency abandons storyboards and slides and physically acts out a concept for an advertising campaign. After viewing the scene, a newspaper sales staff decided to emulate the on-screen technique in a presentation to a local appliance dealership. The dealership not only bought the concept, but also wound up doubling its expenditures with the paper!
- The "15,000 cars" bet in the Michael Keaton film *Gung Ho* led us to set a similarly aggressive goal at one of our companies. As in the movie, the goal was just missed— but the results were so much improved that, like the Japanese automotive executive in the film, we paid up.
- The practice of giving the best sales leads to the best sales closers, as advocated by tough-guy Alec Baldwin in *Glengarry Glen Ross*, led us to re-examine lead allotments at one of our sales divisions. (We didn't adopt Baldwin's onerous philosophy or methods, but discussing the movie helped us uncover issues underlying declining sales production.)
- We used *Twelve O'Clock High* to help a manager who was having difficulty balancing her loyalties to subordinates and her responsibility for achieving the corporate mission. After watching the film, she suggested a realignment of duties that enabled her to redirect her energies so she could spend less time "baby-sitting" and more time coaching the members of her team to record performance.
- We used the 1954 classic *Executive Suite* to launch a major discussion of corporate succession at one of our sub-

sidiaries. The firm was being crippled by a battle over who would become president once the company's founder retired. The film helped each senior manager realize his or her unique contribution to the company. The managers then began functioning as a cooperative team, rather than as competitive individuals. As a result, the company transformed itself and turned the worst year in its history into the following year's best performance ever.

MOVIES ARE UNIQUE TRAINING TOOLS

Movies offer several unique strengths when used as training tools:

1. **Tapes of the movies are readily available and inexpensive (particularly when rented).** Movies won't solve all of your training needs, but they can help you minimize the amount you need to spend on high-cost consultants and high-priced formal training films. Movies are readily accessible from libraries, video stores, videotape clubs and online services.

2. **Training can be individualized. Specific movies can be found to cover almost any topic, but also to match a wide variety of personalities.** The fact that the movies are viewed at leisure and in the security of one's home, surrounded by friends and families, rather than in the company of the boss and one's rivals creates a non-threatening environment for study and reflection. Viewers are less likely to be distracted by pending appointments and phone calls. Our experience suggests that the trainee relishes, rather than resents, training of this type.

3. **Major-release movies are engaging in a way that most traditional training films are not.** Great movies, with their

often huge budgets, are produced to high production standards. They feature well-crafted dialogue, great acting, stirring soundtracks, astonishing special effects and exquisite cinematography. Think about that in comparison to the typical training film. If you work for a large corporation, you've been there: sitting in a sterile room surrounded by your colleagues, all of you part of yet another corporate training-film session featuring yet another reiteration of paradigm theory or another "creativity" session presented in a less than creative way. The training film probably shows another group of people sitting in a sterile room, notepads and laptops in front of them, listening to a management guru discussing the topic *de jour.* When the video ends, the lights come on and you notice that you aren't the only one whose eyes are reopening. In fact, you hear a huge yawn being stifled by one of your colleagues.

This scene is repeated hundreds of times every working day in hundreds of office buildings across the country and around the world—and it gives training a bad name. A major premise of this book is that *training is too important to entrust to traditional training films,* which can be mind-numbingly dull, however important their content.

Good movies are compelling and memorable, capitalizing on story-telling as a time-honored form of teaching and learning.

4. **Movies show the value of form as well as content in dealing with business and leadership situations.** Leadership in shaping organizations and handling crisis is dramatized by the rhetoric of well-scripted actors in productions such as *Hoosiers, Henry V, The Efficiency Expert, Apollo 13, Other People's Money* and *Zulu.* Some movies also depict specific sales presentations, advertising con-

cepts and marketing techniques that can help stir creativity and serve as teaching aids for both ethics and effective salesmanship. These include *The Agency, The Arrangement, The Coca-Cola Kid, Tin Men, Glengarry Glen Ross, The Picture-Show Man, Crazy People, Big* and *Nothing in Common.*

5. **Top-flight films can be inspiring.** A broad range of movies dealing with sports, warfare, politics and invention can help instill or reinforce the sense of mission for business organizations, their managers and their employees. Films such as *Hoosiers, Henry V, The Story of Alexander Graham Bell, Working Girl* and *Hobson's Choice* create a sense of faith that hard work, creativity, persistence and integrity *do* pay off.

6. **Movies enable lessons to be learned in a way that encourages free-flowing discussion.** We have invariably found that employees who are intimidated when it comes to challenging "the boss" on a real-world business opinion have few reservations discussing the same issue in the leveling context of "movie talk." Asking an employee what she would have done had she faced Tess McGill's dilemmas in *Working Girl* is significantly less threatening (and more productive) than asking what she plans to do in a real situation, involving real people in your very real workplace. Once dilemmas have been discussed in the context of the movie, however, it is easy to turn a theoretical discussion into effective workplace action.

A PERSPECTIVE ON BUSINESS IN THE MOVIES

In addition to their value in teaching practical business lessons, the movies also serve a sociological function. The characterization of business, business people and business practice on screen tells us much about popular attitudes toward business in our time.

Though vital to the well-being of any society, business and business people have not fared as well in the movies as have soldiers, political leaders and religious figures. Films frequently depict business as a destructive force that is conspiratorial in nature and unethical. *Norma Rae, The China Syndrome, Wall Street, Silkwood* and *Network,* among many others, show corrupt, impersonal and predatory companies. These "evil empires" are usually headed by obsessive-compulsive executives who lie, cheat, steal and flatter their way to riches, while ripping off their employees, stockholders, customers and communities. It is arguable that such companies are more common on screen than off. If so, the reason is simple: when business performs responsibly—reliably delivering goods and services, treating employees and customers fairly, and supporting its communities and shareholders—there's no drama in it. Indeed, we take for granted that good companies at least try to do these things. But there's little drama in business as usual. The drama comes when rules are violated, people are mistreated and greed substitutes for honest profit. Just as we expect the sun to rise each morning, most workers go through their careers expecting—or at least hoping—that their companies—and ideally, their jobs—will be there the next day. If things go wrong, it must be because a cheating, conniving, greedy, tyrannical, psychopathic boss forgot his duty to shareholders, employees and society. Such villains and issues are the stuff of conflict; conflict is the stuff of drama; and drama is what movies are about. We hate "the bad guys" and we are delighted when, in the *reel* world, they get their comeuppance. Consequently, rats and scuz-bags are common on the screen. *Wall Street's* Gordon Gekko, Mr. Potter in *It's a Wonderful Life, Network's* Diana Christiansen, Demi Moore's character in *Disclosure,* the swindling Carl of *Ghost,* and Bill Murray's heartless broadcast executive in *Scrooged* are among the most detestable.

But even the most anti-business movies can be excellent teaching tools. Films that reflect public fears, suspicions and concerns about corporate practices help sensitize organizations to potentially damaging criticisms. As a popular medium, movies—like newspaper stories and television reports—can arouse and focus negative public opinion on business practices. When serious movies examine abusive corporate practices, headlines and investigations follow, as they did, for example, in the wake of *Wall Street* (insider trading), *Silkwood* (whistle blowing), *Roger & Me* (corporate downsizing and job exporting), and *The China Syndrome* (safety at nuclear power plants). Whether or not such movies are fair or complete in their portrayals of business practices, their influence goes far beyond theaters. Politicians, journalists, employees and shareholders watch such movies—and so should you. An awareness of what's going on at the movies in terms of workplace issues can provide employers with an early warning system and enable them to take voluntary action to prevent or correct problems before they are hit with labor unrest, consumer boycotts or unwanted government regulation.

The "business is evil" subtext of many movies set in the corporate world applies mostly to Big Business. In contrast, Small Business is usually depicted admiringly. Big Business is often stereotyped in films as bureaucratic, arrogant, soulless and anti-competitive. Small Business, however, is usually depicted as highly competitive, visionary and, for the entrepreneur, liberating. If Big Business is sometimes shown setting the odds in its own favor, Small Business will be shown overcoming those odds. We admire the title character in *Mildred Pierce* as she scrimps and saves her money while waiting tables; overcomes myriad financial, operational and marketing obstacles; and finally winds up as president of her own commercial bakery. Notable among other movies that celebrate Small Business are the charming *Kidco*, the poignant *My Beautiful Launderette*, the award-winning *Hobson's Choice*, and the ubiquitous Christmas classic *It's a Wonderful Life*.

There are, of course, dozens of movies that feature thoughtful, brilliant, heroic Big Business leaders, including the subjects of *The Story of Alexander Graham Bell*, *Lloyd's of London*, *Dispatch from Reuters*, *Young Thomas Edison* and *Edison the Man*. Among other examples, Spencer Tracy plays an admirable technology consultant in *Desk Set;* Hal Holbrook represents a thoughtful and principled stockbroker in *Wall Street;* and Joanna Cassidy is cast as an effective and supportive mentor in *Don't Tell Mom the Babysitter's Dead*.

As in real life, most business people in the movies are neither "good guys" nor "bad guys." Many are seen in minor, workaday roles: bank officers who grant or turn down loans, store managers who assist the star with a purchase, convenience-store operators held up at gun point, car dealers closing a deal, bar owners serving as sounding boards for customers. These folks simply go about their business on screen, helping to move the plot along—often without a single line of dialogue.

In addition to heroes, villains and backdrop players, the movies abound with business eccentrics. These are as quirky as they are wealthy: Burt Lancaster as the mystic, comet-chasing oil magnate in *Local Hero;* Danny DeVito as "Larry the Liquidator" in *Other People's Money;* Mr. Ball, the paternalistic shoe manufacturer, in *The Efficiency Expert;* the toy company CEOs in *Big* and *Toys*; the wagering financiers in *Trading Places*; and Orson Wells as the eponymous newspaper baron, Citizen Kane. If some of these characters come from real life and others are thinly veiled fictions, the films that present them invariably focus on their eccentricity, rather than their substance. For example, while eccentricity was certainly a trait of the inventive Howard Hughes, it becomes his defining characteristic in films like *Tucker* and *Melvin and Howard*.

Movies not only alter our perceptions to create a sense of conflict and drama, but also to capture the spirit of their times. During the Great Depression, for example, the nation sought both the causes and the cures for its economic woes. Business was a hot topic for the movies. In some films (several of Frank Capra's come to mind), businessmen were cast as the cause and perpetuators of economic catastrophe. More often, however, movies of the 1930s celebrated business people as models of innovation and leadership that would propel nations to new prosperity, as in *Lloyd's of London, The Story of Alexander Graham Bell, Dispatch from Reuters, The Great Ziegfeld, The House of Rothschild, Union Pacific* and the Edison films.

As America moved out of the Depression and into World War II, business-related movies began to show examples of labor and management dropping their differences to work together in the war effort, as in the 1942 John Wayne-Randolph Scott vehicle *Pittsburgh* and in 1944's *An American Romance*. When the war was over, the movies again switched gears, moving to an examination of the practices which led to war-time profiteering (as in 1948's *All My Sons*).

As Americans reached new heights of prosperity in the 1950s, they began questioning workplace values. Films like *Death of a Salesman* and *The Man in the Grey Flannel Suit* showed American white-collar workers coming apart as pressures mounted and their companies' demands increased. With the rise of computers in the workplace, office workers feared losing their jobs to automation—fears that the Katherine Hepburn-Spencer Tracy film *Desk Set* tried to dispel with romantic charm.

During the 1960s and 1970s, business fell victim on screen to the same type of Vietnam-inspired disillusionment America was exhibiting with most of its institutions. The business world was mocked or bitterly skewered in films as disparate as *Salesman, Putney Swope* and *How to Succeed in Business Without Really Trying.*

During the 1980s and early years of the 1990s—amid takeover fever on Wall Street and downsizing fears in back offices and on assembly lines, America's screens were filled with depictions of greed and corporate insensitivity in films like *Wall Street, Roger & Me, Barbarians at the Gates* and *End of the Line.*

A sub-genre of the business movie is the labor movie, which champions the cause and celebrates the leaders of the unfairly exploited "working man" (or in the case of films like *Norma Rae, Working Girl* and *9 to 5*, "working woman"). Again, such films reflect the issues of the day, even though they may depict labor struggles from a previous period, as in *Hoffa, F.I.S.T., The Killing Floor, Blue Collar, Newsies,* and the French films *Germinal, L'Argent* and *Coup Pour Coup (Blow for Blow).*

With the women's movement of the 1970s calling the tune, Hollywood danced, creating heroines like Melanie Griffith's in *Working Girl,* the three office workers in *9 to 5,* Sally Field's labor organizer in *Norma Rae* and Meryl Streep's whistle-blowing nuclear-plant worker in *Silkwood.* The films depicted overworked, underpaid, stressed-out women battling harassment in the workplace while trying to balance work, family and social life. Ironically, while Hollywood has often portrayed working women as victims (and sometimes, as in *Network* and *Disclosure*, villains), it has produced few films showing women performing admirably and effectively in top executive roles. Joan Crawford in *Mildred Pierce* is an exception in terms of the way she builds and runs her commercial bakery, but she is a lamentable role model because her success costs her any chance of finding love, happiness or gratitude. Among movies featuring businesswomen, *Hobson's Choice* stands out. It presents a strong, hard-working, talented, independent, no-nonsense woman entrepreneur. She succeeds in building a cobblery on the basis of her will, brains, devotion to customer service, eye to fashion and eye for talent!

Regardless of the era, some business sectors seem never to receive a "fair shake" in the movies. Advertising, for example, is almost never shown as a necessary element in the marketing of goods. The focus, instead, is on the actual practices (invariably exaggerated) of agency owners and creatives. Advertising is sometimes dealt with in relatively benign comedic scenes, as in *How to Succeed in Business Without Really Trying, Mr. Blandings Builds His Dream House,* the Tom Hanks-Jackie Gleason film *Nothing in Common,* and Dudley Moore's *Crazy People.* There are, however, bitterly sinister depictions, such as those in *Putney Swope* and *How to Get a Head in Advertising.* In all cases advertising gets no respect even though, in the real world, no business—particularly the movie business—can hope to bring its product successfully to market without effective advertising or alternative promotional assistance.

In drawing practical business lessons from business-related movies, viewers must look beyond a movie's social commentary and examine the onscreen practices with a critical eye. The viewer must ask, for example, what is actually going on behind the scenes? We are told that an on-screen deal is shady or illegal, often without knowing the details of the law or the practice. This requires us to evaluate scenes in the context of business reality rather than screen fantasy. What, for example, are the specifics of the violations of security laws engaged in by Gordon Gekko and Bud Fox in *Wall Street?* How exactly does "Larry the Liquidator" determine the feasibility of acquiring the wire and cable company in *Other People's Money?* The movies almost always ask us to suspend disbelief in order to create a sense of drama. As management viewers, however, we cannot give up critical thinking. Instead, we must look at practices and ask, "What is really going on here? Is that really the way this happens in the real world?" As management viewers, we sometimes need to fill in the blanks, too. We may be told, for example, that a proxy fight is going on in *Other People's Money* or *Executive Suite.* The movies cut short the mechanics and "boring" details about proxies and show us only the fight. Because *Management Goes to the Movies*™ guides are designed to broaden your business knowledge, develop your business perspective and heighten your business performance, we try to fill in the relevant business details by providing, as an example, glossaries explaining technical terms and break-out boxes that explain what would be going on behind the scenes in a real proxy fight.

MANAGEMENT GOES TO THE MOVIES™ GUIDES

In each *Management Goes to the Movies*™ guide you'll find capsule descriptions and analysis of four or more films that illustrate key business principles. Some of the movies, like

The Efficiency Expert, Tucker: The Man and His Dream, Gates of Heaven, The Story of Alexander Graham Bell and *Gung Ho,* deal directly with business problems: cost control, regulation, new product development, motivation, patents and labor relations. Others, including *Zulu, The Godfather* trilogy, *The Wizard of Oz, Moby Dick* and *Hoosiers,* illustrate organizational, leadership and operational skills in non-business settings. A third set of films, including *Mildred Pierce* and *Don't Tell Mom the Babysitter's Dead,* features business settings and offers business lessons, but business is not the central focus of the films. Another set of movies focuses specifically on the ethics of business and includes *Glengarry Glen Ross, Save the Tiger, All My Sons* and *Wall Street.*

Movies in each guide have been selected for their entertainment value, the quality of their management lessons and their power to stir meaningful discussion. The movies represent the entire range of story types: light comedy, drama, action, and tragedy. Some (like *Hoosiers)* are based on original screenplays, while others (including *Henry V, The Bridge on the River Kwai* and *Other People's Money)* have been adapted from stage plays and novels.

The guides are designed for self-study or assignment for private viewing. There are two reasons for this: first, copyright restrictions preclude legal viewing of videotapes in group settings outside the home for purposes other than entertainment; and second, trainers must be sensitive to the broad range of personalities and tolerance levels found in the workplace. In private life, many employees may decline to attend certain movies as a matter of religious belief or as a means of protesting gratuitous sex, violence and objectionable language. Consequently, required attendance at any group showing of a movie with an industry rating above PG is risky in the modern corporate environment. Also, older movies in particular may include minor scenes featuring ethnic stereotypes that many employees may find objectionable and offensive. Ideally, the motion-picture industry will recognize the corporate-training assets inherent in their films and start releasing "edited for business" versions of key films in the same way it releases time- and content-altered versions for broadcast and airline viewing. In the absence of such versions, we have provided the official Motion Picture Producers Association ratings (G, PG, PG-13 and R) for every movie used in the MGTTM series. When needed, we also alert you to content that might be objectionable on grounds other than those covered by the MPPA rating system. Finally, we've added a "Business Value Rating" (BVR) using one to five attaché cases. (Five is tops and no movie is used unless it rates at least three.) These ratings represent our judgment of the depth, breadth and significance of a film's training lessons. (Movies receive *five* attaché cases *only* if they are considered outstanding for both their business lessons and their entertainment quality.)

Movies provide valuable training material, but they cannot be viewed in a training vacuum—training *context* must be established. The lessons must be framed and viewers must have a basic understanding of how movies work. Before sending a video home with managers, remind them that most movies are designed to entertain, not teach. Popular films are constructed to produce responses of horror, delight, laughter, revulsion and sympathy. Emphasize that filmmakers distill and enhance situations, utilizing suspense, exaggeration, satire, tragedy and comic juxtaposition, to keep viewers engaged. Don't be afraid to point out the obvious: that "reel" life is seldom real—no matter how believable it may seem when you are watching a movie unfold.

In the movies, facts are often distorted; time is almost

always condensed; and details are often left to the imagination. In the movies, the "good guys" and "bad guys" are usually a bit better or worse than the people we deal with in the real world. In the movies, we are made aware of all relevant actions and motives—good or bad—of the principle characters. In real life, of course, we seldom have that information. Most of the time we don't know why bosses, peers and subordinates act the way they do. A bad decision may be due simply to someone having a bad day. Errors in judgment are usually caused by banal factors of distraction, indifference, stress, misinformation, ambivalence or true stupidity, rather than malice. Unlike in the movies, our co-workers have not been typecast as heroes, villains or psychopaths. Most of them are simply trying to do their jobs, get through the day and get on with their lives as best they can. Ideally, by studying examples of good and bad practices on screen, you will be able to do a better job, feel better at the end of the day and add a little interest to the life you're getting on with.

The movies tell us not only that there are good guys and bad guys, but also that there is a *problem* and, in most cases, that its *cause is known*. In real business, that's seldom the case. Instead we have to *discover* the problem and investigate its *probable causes*. And because life is longer than a movie, we don't usually solve problems as quickly—we can choose to deal with a problem tomorrow, or next week, or next year, or not at all. If we operated our companies along the lines of movies, all problems would be resolved within two or three hours and, ideally, there would be a happy ending. In real life, we can take more time to make good decisions, but we can also procrastinate, allowing small problems to fester until we have no time left in which to solve them. In that case, our real life "movie" becomes a disaster epic!

SEND US A MANAGER WHO GOES TO THE MOVIES!

A famous advertising series for International Paper Company featured CEOs of major companies expounding on the concept, "Send me a man who reads." (Today, no doubt, those ads would say send me a "person" or "manager" who reads!) The CEOs invariably noted that serious readers were exposed to more knowledge, kept up with current events, were aware of more ideas and were better able to express their thoughts. In today's multimedia environment, many of the advantages of hiring an avid reader are complemented by hiring a person who enthusiastically and critically watches movies. We routinely ask entry-level job applicants not only about their recent reading, but also if they've seen any good movies lately. Both questions test an applicant's depth of observation and thought, as well as his or her ability to express thoughts clearly. Applicants who can discuss books and movies with insight and intelligence tend to demonstrate that same insight and intelligence in the workplace. That's why we say, "Send us a manager who goes to the movies"—and send more movies home with managers.

LEADERSHIP:

*The Key to Corporate Performance
And Personal Advancement*

Technical excellence can only carry you so far.

If you want to reach the top, you must transcend specific, task-oriented competence and achieve general, goal-oriented excellence. *You must become a leader.*

Leadership is the quality that makes boardroom generals out of "prairie-dogging" specialists isolated in a field of office cubicles. Your "Yellow Brick Road" to the top involves knowing how to create a vision, instill it in others, delegate effectively, and develop a sense of accountability in others while modeling accountability yourself.

Great leaders share many traits, including those we call "The Magnificent Seven":

1. Leaders have a plan and passionately pursue it.
2. Leaders work hard.
3. Leaders are focused on success.
4. Leaders know how to develop good teams.
5. Leaders have thick skins and are able to bounce back from setbacks.
6. Leaders inspire commitment in others.
7. Leaders challenge the status quo.

The movies in this guide provide examples of what these leadership characteristics look like, both on screen and in the workplace.

Many of a leader's necessary traits are demonstrated in *The Wizard of Oz*, chosen by the American Film Insititute as one of the Top 10 movies of all time; and in *Hoosiers*, selected by *USA Today* readers as their favorite sports movie of all time. Once you've mastered the lessons taught by Dorothy Gale and Coach Norman Dale, you'll not only be ready to lead, but to triumph. On the flip side, leadership demands that you know not only what to do, but also what *not* to do. That's why we've illustrated some of the traps and presented ways to avoid them in chapters dealing with *The Bridge on the River Kwai* and *Moby Dick*.

Leaders come in many forms. They can be "small and meek" like Dorothy or strong and outspoken like Coach Dale. They can attain their leadership roles through brains, compassion or bravery, like the Scarecrow, Tin Man and Lion; or from outstanding technical skill and peer support, like Jimmy Chitwood.

Above all, truly great leaders keep focused on their missions and are tireless in pursuing them. When you master the lessons of *The Wizard of Oz* and *Hoosiers*, you'll be ready to lead your own team to success.

In today's business environment, with its emphasis on self-directed work teams, it is critical to understand that successful organizations must have leadership at all levels and in all operational areas.

With these thoughts in mind, we urge you to start your viewing. Turn down the lights, turn on the VCR, sit back, relax and enjoy some of the most enlightening leadership movies ever produced. After you've watched the movies, read through the guide, consider the discussion questions and think of ways to apply the lessons you learn to your career and within your organization. You'll soon be on your way to becoming the better leader that is within you.

HOOSIERS:

Courting Success in Hoopsville

Coach Dale's (Gene Hackman, center) Huskers wait for instructions during an important game. *Photo credit:* Photofest.

WATCH AND READ IF:

- You need to do a better job of motivating groups of people toward the achievement of specific, short-term goals.

- You work for a small company that competes with big companies.

- You have limited options when it comes to replacing less skilled workers or expanding your staff.

- You have just changed jobs.

- You question the value of teams.

- You believe inspiration is more important than perspiration in achieving success.

HOOSIERS:

Courting Success in Hoopsville

Imagine you've accepted a new job with a small firm. When you arrive, you find the staff in place has been working for weeks on projects that will now be turned over to you. As the new kid on the block, you have to deal with all the old-timers who are anxious to advise you and help you learn how things are done at "their" firm. You know that you'll soon be changing things— the "status quo" is not good enough—and that your changes won't be popular. Going in, your only true friend is the person who hired you. It's a tough situation, but you've been in tough situations before. You have used your methods successfully in previous assignments, including one with a Fortune 500 company. You know they are the best methods for your new assignment, too. You have a schedule to meet. You must minimize distractions and get the company in shape fast. How do you proceed? You might start by considering a few lessons from the classic sports movie, Hoosiers.

Good managers often find themselves in situations involving limited resources; and in *Hoosiers,* Coach Dale's are very limited. Hickory High is small. Dale can barely fill a

HOOSIERS

US (1986): Sports

114 minutes. Color. Available
on videocassette and laserdisc.

Audience Rating: **PG**

CAST LIST

<u>Performer</u>	<u>Character</u>
Gene Hackman	Coach Norman Dale
Barbara Hershey	Myra Fleener
Dennis Hopper	Shooter
Sheb Wooley	Cletus
Fern Parsons	Opal Fleener
Brad Boyle	Whit
Steve Hollar	Rade
Brad Long	Strap
David Neidorf	Everett
Kent Poole	Merle
Wade Schenck	Ollie
Scott Summers	Wick
Maris Valainis	Jimmy
Chelcie Ross	George

Directed by David Anspaugh
Screenplay by Angelo Pizzo

team roster—the Huskers' "sixth man" has to double as ball boy. Like Coach Dale, new managers are often second-guessed by everyone around them. But Dale sticks to his principles and molds the team to perfection. What are his secrets?

COACH DALE'S KEYS TO SUCCESS

- Establish your authority
- Build <u>your</u> team, not somebody else's
- Master the fundamentals
- Maintain discipline
- Make the best of the hand you are dealt
- Don't write anyone off
- Focus on the game, not the fieldhouse
- Be loyal to yourself and your principles
- Develop leadership in others
- Know your competition
- Have faith

Let's look at each of Dale's rules and how he applies them.

#1 ESTABLISH YOUR AUTHORITY

Dale establishes his authority immediately with his peers, with the townspeople and with his team—and he does it in three effective ways.

First, Dale gives short shrift to inquisitors, self-appointed advisors and nosy antagonists. Mess with him, he'll mess with you. He does this with style: he is firm, direct, never strident. When Myra Fleener starts asking unexpected (and uncalled for) questions, he shuts her down. He doesn't have to be interviewed again—and certainly not by her; he already has the job. Later, when the kibitzing townsmen start to tell Dale how to manage the team, he reminds them who's coach by simply saying goodnight and walking away. It's not that Dale is averse to advice or that he won't listen. Throughout the movie he shows that he's a good listener when someone has something significant to say. One of Dale's strengths is his ability to distinguish good and well-intentioned advice (such as Shooter's) from advice that is self-serving and short-sighted (such as George's). Great managers listen when valuable information is being communicated, but they don't waste time on idle chat and armchair quarterbacking.

Second, Dale establishes authority with the team by sharing his vision. He knows it's not enough merely to show his job description and terms of employment. To succeed, his authority must come from the team, from its buy-in to his principles, its acceptance of his plan and its faith in his dedication to his own ideals. Dale states his vision clearly from the start. He tells the team there is more to the game than shooting. The team, he says, must focus on fundamentals and defense. He believes that the five players on the floor must function as a team, a single unit, no player more important than the others. Ultimately, his authority will come from that vision, not the circumstances of his hiring.

Third, when his authority is challenged by a team member, he responds with full force, tossing the player off the team. He has, in the words of Chairman Mao, "killed one to terrorize ten thousand" (or in Dale's case, his remaining five players).

#2 BUILD <u>YOUR</u> TEAM, NOT SOMEONE ELSE'S

Myra Fleener wants the Coach to build a team without Jimmy Chitwood. Smilin' George, the acting coach, and his kibitzing buddies want a team built *with* Jimmy and around particular styles of play. Dale immediately recognizes Myra and George as internal competitors who want him to back off from doing his job *his* way because it gets in the way of their own goals.

Dale knows he must be particularly wary of "friendly" helpers like George. George will always be a 15–10 season coach; he needs Dale to validate his mediocrity. George and his pals want to minimize necessary change and will seek to hinder the new coach whenever they can. The coach avoids useless discussion with them and shares his plans only with true allies.

It would be easy for the Coach to go with the flow, appeasing everyone who would settle for a repeat of Hickory's previous and mediocre 15–10 season. If Dale builds that kind of team—a team of so-so winners—he'll have plenty of fans in Hickory; but he doesn't want fans, he wants excellence. In choosing his management team in Hickory, Dale does what every successful manager does: he finds lieutenants who want to help him achieve *his* goals, not theirs. He puts together a team of helpers who believe in him and his abilities: Mr. Butcher, Shooter, Cletis, Ms. Fleener's mother and, eventually, Myra herself. The key to developing strong management teams lies in identifying aides who want to help you achieve your goals, not compromise them.

#3 MASTER THE FUNDAMENTALS

In the workplace, as in the gym, practicing basic skills increases the confidence a team has in its abilities and reinforces the importance of teamwork.

Dale is remorseless in drilling his team in the "boring" aspects of the game: the basics of ball-handling, dribbling, defense and endurance. Shooting the ball is secondary. He knows that winning can come in many ways. It's easier to outscore a team whose score can be kept low. It's easier to win a game if an opponent is worn out before you are. It's easier to win a game if you can out-run, out-dribble, out-steal and out-pass an opponent as a means to outscoring him. When Dale takes over the team, the acting coach has been running 50–minute drills, with the team practicing for 20 minutes, breaking for 10 and practicing for 20 more, and with most of the time spent in shooting and scrimmages. Dale's practices run for at least two hours and most of the time is spent on endurance and ball-handling exercises.

#4 MAINTAIN DISCIPLINE

Coach Dale sticks to a proven plan and maintains discipline. Being uncompromising is part of his discipline. By refusing to compromise, he underscores the importance he places on his job.

The mastery of fundamentals is worthwhile, but only if it is applied in the real world of "the game." In their first matchup, the Huskers fall apart on the floor, despite locker room review of the basics. When the crowd starts booing and urging players to shoot before they complete Dale's requisite four passes, the players go with the crowd, abandoning Dale's training. Eventually he benches one player, Rade, who starts shooting (and hitting) when he should be following Dale's passing regimen. When foul trouble leaves the team with only four players on the floor, Rade starts to re-enter the game only to be told to sit down. Dale will end the game with only four men on the floor. The crowd boos the coach, but Dale sticks to his guns. Only players who are team players will see action. The team loses, but the coach has made his point. He knows he will win more games with a disciplined team that sticks to the game plan than with one that breaks up into one-player shows.

#5 MAKE THE BEST OF THE HAND YOU ARE DEALT

Dale has extremely limited resources. There are only 63 boys in the whole school and fewer than ten are likely, under any circumstance, to come out for basketball. The best player, Jimmy Chitwood, may sit out the season or choose to play for another school. The coach knows that, except for Jimmy, he has no recruiting prospects. It's not going to be easy to find replacements if a player quits, is injured or is thrown off the team. Dale has to use the players he has and he has to keep them fit and healthy. That's why he spends so much time on endurance exercises. Lacking the ability to rest his players on the bench (he only has a two-man bench and it's weak), he has to keep his starters on the floor whenever possible. That means they have to be in top condition. In a late tournament game, Shooter's son is injured when he crashes into a trophy case. Instinct prompts Dale to send the boy back into the game, injured or not, with a few quick stitches and a bandage. Before the boy re-enters the game, however, Dale has a change of heart. Perhaps he is haunted by memories of the time he hit a player in frustration, putting his obsession with winning ahead of the player's welfare. More likely, however, Dale realizes that winning today's game and losing a key player for the rest of the tournament is as short-sighted strategically as it is ethically. Dale may need the player more in the future than at the present.

Dale's hand would be greatly improved if he could play Jimmy Chitwood. Chitwood is an ace, but he's not in Dale's deck (nor up his sleeve) when the season starts. Dale can't count on Jimmy coming on board. If Jimmy opts in, as he eventually does, Dale will have a better hand to play and the team will be stronger. Without Jimmy, however, Dale must make the team itself a star, playing the cards he holds, not those he wishes he had.

Dale fosters the team concept by standing up for his players during the "pep session from hell." Dale introduces his team at the first school assembly of the season. Instead of saluting the team, the students start chanting, "We want Jimmy! We want Jimmy!" The coach stops the chant and tells the students he had hoped the team would be appreciated for who they are, not who they are not. "*This* is your team!" he says as his players stand stunned before the silent, chastened fans.

#6 DON'T WRITE ANYONE OFF

Your team is only as strong as its weakest player. Neglecting your slowest staff member may leave you in the lurch at the very time you need to score. Managers who spend time coaching *every* member of the team improve their chances of survival during crisis.

Coach Dale knows he can't afford to write off any

player. Circumstances could put any of his players in a crucial, game-deciding situation. Remember that scene in the regionals of the tournament when the Huskers are plagued by foul trouble in a tight game? Dale is left with his weakest player, Ollie, on the foul line. If Ollie makes the shot, the Huskers win and advance in the tournament. Otherwise, they go to the showers for the last time. Ollie, of course, makes the shot—a shot that is not a product of luck, but of the hours of practice Dale has spent drilling Ollie and his teammates in fundamentals. What if Ollie had been written off, ignored by the coach? The outcome, predictably, would have been a loss.

Imagine a situation in which one of your key accounts is on the line, but your chief account executive is out because of serious illness, an accident or a death in her immediate family. You may have to send in an assistant, an Ollie, to call on the account. Can you afford not to have an Ollie trained to do his best? Even if he's not a star, even if his sales call is not as effective as the star's, it must be good enough to save the account—or at least get you into an overtime situation in which your star will again be able to play.

Ollie isn't the only "loser" in whom Dale invests effort. He salvages Shooter, a man the entire town has written off as a good-for-nothing drunkard. But Dale recognizes Shooter's formidable knowledge of the game. He also knows that Shooter's alcoholism is a distraction to Shooter's son's performance. If Shooter can be shaped up, Dale will have gained a useful ally and a great assistant coach. He will also have a more stable player in Shooter's son, who will be able to focus full attention on his game instead of his dad. Dale's investment in Shooter pays off when Shooter, with a helpful prompt from his son, coaches the team to a crucial victory.

#7 FOCUS ON THE GAME, NOT THE FIELDHOUSE

Coach Dale knows that his team's greatest fear may be fear of success. Nobody really expects Hickory to win the state championship—it's a surprise that they are even in the finals. If the Huskers simply manage not to embarrass themselves, they can make all kinds of excuses for losing: small town, small school, small players, great effort. Dale sees the fear in his team and works to overcome it. Throughout the tournament, he urges the team to focus on the game they are playing, not the next game and certainly not the championship. He keeps them busy practicing, not only to build their confidence, but also to distract them from their fear.

Dale also makes his team focus on the realities of the game, not the phantoms of the gigantic fieldhouse in which it will be played. Dale is fighting not only his players' "fear of success," but also an intimidation factor. Intimidation factors are always at work when small, out-of-the-way organizations find themselves in head-to-head competition with giant enterprises. The Huskers will be playing the championship game in a fieldhouse that can seat the entire population of Hickory many times over. They are like upstart Apple vs. mature IBM. The Huskers will be playing a big city team that is used to playing before large crowds in large arenas. The coach uses concrete examples, not just words, to help the team relax. He walks the boys around the fieldhouse and has them measure the playing floor. It's the same size as the one in Hickory. He then has them measure the distance from the floor to the basket. Same as in Hickory. He drills them in fundamentals one last time—just as he would before any other game. He removes the fear of Goliath and allows his Davids to go forth confidently.

#8 BE LOYAL TO YOURSELF AND YOUR PRINCIPLES

Dale not only talks the talk, but walks the walk. Time and again, Dale's actions demonstrate the value of staying loyal to your principles. We first see it when he keeps Rade on the bench and plays with only four players. Later, when the townspeople meet to vote on firing him as coach, Dale offers no apologies. He has done his best so no apologies are required. Despite the pressure from the fans, the doubts of Cletis, the doubts of the players and, unquestionably, his own occasional self-doubts, Dale stands firm. His determination eventually wins over not only Myra Fleener, but also Jimmy Chitwood. By the end of the film, even George is cheering again.

Former President Lyndon Johnson once described the art of consensus as "forcing everybody to take sides until they wind up on yours." In *Hoosiers*, Dale does just that.

#9 DEVELOP LEADERSHIP IN OTHERS

In order to build Shooter's confidence, Dale has himself thrown out of a game forcing Shooter to coach the team to game's end. As the boys huddle around Shooter awaiting advice, Shooter freezes up. Sensing his dad's fear, Shooter's son asks him a question about one of the opposing players. Prompted in this way, Shooter answers the question and, his jitters gone, begins coaching. Shooter calls the winning play and is carried off the floor on the team's shoulders.

Dale has not only succeeded in developing Shooter as a coach, but also in developing leadership in Shooter's son who, in a previous scene, had refused to help his dad in a similar situation. By the end of the movie, every player on the team has demonstrated leadership by encouraging a fellow player, taking personal responsibility for the outcome of a game or shoring up team spirit in a moment of doubt.

By the last minutes of the final game, the entire team has earned the right to challenge Dale—and he has learned to listen to them in return. In the final huddle, Dale calls for Rade to take the last shot, expecting that the opposing team will be over-guarding Jimmy. The team sees it differently. Jimmy should take the last shot; he's why they're in the final game. Looking directly at the coach, Jimmy says simply, "I'll make it." We hope he will, and Dale hopes so, too. In saying "I'll make it," Jimmy has exhibited a great trait of leaders: he has taken personal responsibility for outcomes. Dale, meanwhile, has also mastered a new major leadership trait. He has delegated decision-making and shown that he knows when to let the team make the call.

#10 KNOW YOUR COMPETITION INTIMATELY

Once you've gotten your own company in shape, there's the other company to consider. Just as you have to know your own strengths and weaknesses, you have to know the competition's.

Coach Dale takes advantage of Shooter's knowledge of the opposing teams: their gyms, their playing styles, their fans. He also demands that his players gather their own intelligence in ways that help them understand their opponents. In one game, Dale tells a player he wants to know what kind of gum an opponent is chewing. When the Husker later fouls out, he tells the coach from the end of the bench, "Dentyne."

Knowing the kind of gum your opponent chews will get you close enough to know a lot more. Management guru

Michael Porter of Harvard Business School has demonstrated in his books on the topic that competitive analysis is not just a matter of analyzing the other team. You also have to analyze several other factors, including customer behavior. If you know your customers better than your competition does, you'll be better able to respond to their needs. "Know what kind of gum they chew" is a good slogan, worthy of a place on any company's wall.

#11 HAVE FAITH

Finally, Coach Dale has faith. So, eventually, do the townspeople. So does the team. Their faith is not just a matter of the prayers said before each game. Dale himself seems to tolerate, rather than demonstrate, faith in a deity, but he shows ample faith in his team and his lieutenants. He stands by Shooter when he falls off the wagon. He stands by Rade when he punches out a player who insults the coach. He has faith at the end in Jimmy Chitwood's statement that he'll make the final shot in the championship game. That core faith in one's direction, one's beliefs about the best course of action, and one's faith in the commitment and dedication of the team is essential to staying the course that leads to victory.

Minute by minute, *Hoosiers* offers managers great lessons in style, practice and principle that can be adapted to a broad range of business situations. In addition, *Hoosiers* offers inspiration. It's a movie to watch when your team is in the doldrums, facing overwhelming odds against success, or when you as team leader are facing moments of self-doubt. Yes, it's predictable: we know the Huskers will

Six Tips On Monitoring
Your Competition—Legally

1. **Read their annual report.** If they don't do the fancy ones, get a copy of their filings from your Secretary of State's office. If they aren't a corporation, there won't be any filings or annual reports; but you might be able to get copies of their employee newsletters or utilize clipping services to monitor coverage your competition receives in the media.

2. **Test their products.** You can't compete against what you don't use. If their product has a great feature, you'll need to match it, offer an improvement or offer a different feature of equal perceived value. If their product has a weak feature, the best way to discover it is to use the product yourself.

3. **Poll <u>their</u> customers.** In many businesses the customer pool for competitors is the same as yours. Your customers are their potential customers; theirs are yours. So have a survey firm poll that customer pool and rank various vendors on key customer service and product questions. Find out where you stand. Find out what customers like and don't like about both you and your competitors.

4. **Count cars on their parking lot and people going in and out of their doors.** Once you've done that, you have a basis for comparing their traffic to your traffic.

5. **If they have one, visit their Internet site monthly.** You'll be amazed by what you can gather from your competitor's Internet site that the competitor would never release elsewhere. We know of one publishing company that monitored another's site to see how many mentions a key geographic area had received in the competitor's publications during the previous six months. Finding few mentions of some areas, the monitoring company decided to seek more subscribers in the areas being under-served by the competitor. Another example: book publishers can now go to **amazon.com's** website and instantly find out where their sales rank among more than a million titles. If you have a copy of your competitor's list of books, you can check out each of those titles and find out what's moving and what's not.

6. **Monitor their advertising.** Obviously, you must monitor their prices, but that's not what we mean here. You can determine easily where your competitor is placing ads, how many they are placing, the size of the ads, and whether or not they are paying for color or premium positions. This can help you determine their advertising budget; note increases and decreases in it; and, using industry formulas that relate ad budgets to revenue, get an idea of their overall marketing budget. Significant reductions in ad size, frequency and color can signal tight budgets at your competition.

> ### The Real Life Story of
> ### "The Little Team that Could"
>
> *Hoosiers* is based on the real-life story of the 1954 Milan Indians basketball team, representing the smallest school in history to win the Indiana High School Basketball Championship.
>
> Milan, a school of 161 students, defeated Muncie Central, a long-time Indiana basketball powerhouse and a school more than ten times larger than Milan. Milan was led by a player named Bobby Plump, the role model for Jimmy Chitwood and a player often described as the "best pure shooter" in the state's basketball history. Just as Jimmy Chitwood is based on a real character, Coach Norman Dale and his coaching style are often compared to another Hoosier sports legend: Coach Bob "The General" Knight, a noted disciplinarian and "team-approach" leader who has coached three Indiana University teams to the NCAA Championship.

win; we know Ollie will make that free throw; we know Jimmy will make the final shot in the final game; and we know for sure that before the credits roll, Coach Dale and Myra will be an item. It's all as corny as an Indiana August. And yet it's all done so well that it transcends its predictability. The acting is extraordinary, the photography stunning, and Jerry Goldsmith's soundtrack should be on every manager's tape of motivational music. Listening to it, one hears the pounding of balls on the gym floor, smells the crisp air of late autumn and early winter, and knows

> **USA TODAY Readers Vote *Hoosiers*
> #1 Sports Movie of All Time**
>
> In July 1998, readers of *USA TODAY* voted *Hoosiers* their favorite sports movie of all time. A total of 10,500 readers responded to the poll and *Hoosiers* showed up on 62 percent of the ballots, edging out *Field of Dreams* (60%) and *The Natural* (55%).

that whatever project one is working on, success lies just down the road.

DISCUSSION QUESTIONS

1. What are the fundamental skills—the core competencies—of your business? Of your job? When was the last time you thought about those fundamentals or worked to improve your skill level relating to those fundamentals? (If you think you've mastered all the fundamentals, ask yourself: can I shoot perfectly, dribble without error and pass with pinpoint accuracy?)
2. How might you apply the concept of "focus on the game, not the fieldhouse" to a real situation in your business? What actions—like measuring the fieldhouse—might help you achieve that kind of focus?
3. Not everyone performs well under managers like Coach Dale—though everyone must perform FOR Coach Dale. Coach Dale has found one good way to manage

and motivate those who choose to play for him and accept his style of management. Can you imagine a style of management that would be almost the exact opposite of Dale's? What would the principle points be? Would such a management style produce a winning effort?

4. What kind of gum does your top competitor chew? More important, what kind of gum do your most important customers chew?

5. If your company were a movie, what would its soundtrack be like? Would it have the inspiring and evocative qualities of the one in *Hoosiers*? Do you need a new tune?

6. How have you demonstrated faith in your team and its mission today?

THE WIZARD OF OZ:

Finding the Magic Wand Within

Dorothy and her "heartless, brainless, gutless" friends become a powerful team that carries out its mission successfully. *Photo credit:* Photofest.

WATCH AND READ IF:

- You doubt your own capabilities or credentials for a job.

- You expect the worst from your subordinates.

- You have difficulty delegating tasks and authority.

- You need to build up your personal presence.

- You suffer from "paralysis by analysis."

THE WIZARD OF OZ:

Finding the Magic Wand Within

You've probably seen The Wizard of Oz *a gazillion times. (If you haven't, what planet are you from?) The American Film Institute rated* Oz *the sixth-best film ever made. We think it's also one of the Top 10 leadership training films of all time—a fact recognized years ago by Lou Tice, one of the nation's top corporate trainers. Tice, a former championship high-school football coach in the state of Washington, built The Pacific Institute by counseling companies and their managers on ways to introduce positive wizards (good mentors) into their lives, while expelling negative wizards (anyone who tries to make you feel bad about yourself or, worse, tells you that you are incapable of success). Tice argued that Dorothy was a great leader because she "took a guy with no brains, one with no heart and one with no courage" and melded them into an effective team that successfully accomplished its mission.*

More recently Oz*'s lessons were extolled in the business bestseller* The Oz Principle *by Roger Connors, Tom Smith and Craig Hickman. They base their analysis on L. Frank Baum's book rather than the movie it inspired. They used the* Oz *story as a metaphor for issues of accountability, arguing that Dorothy and her team succeeded only after they stopped blaming others for their problems, stopped waiting for someone to wave a magic wand and started*

THE WIZARD OF OZ

US (1939): Musical/Fantasy/Dance

101 minutes. Available
on videocassette and laserdisc.

Audience Rating : **NR**

CAST LIST

<u>Performer</u>	<u>Character</u>
Judy Garland	Dorothy
Ray Bolger	Hunk/The Scarecrow
Bert Lahr	Zeke/The Cowardly Lion
Jack Haley	Hickory/The Tin Woodsman
Billie Burke	Glinda
Margaret Hamilton	Miss Gulch The Wicked Witch
Charley Grapewin	Uncle Henry
Clara Blandick	Auntie Em
Pat Walsh	Nikko
Frank Morgan	Professor Marvel The Wizard The Guard The Coachman
The Singer Midgets	Munchkins
Mitchell Lewis	Monkey Officer
Terry the Dog	Toto

Produced by Mervyn LeRoy
Directed by Victor Fleming (and King Vidor)
Written by Noel Langley
Based on the novel by L. Frank Baum

taking responsibility for their own destinies. As you'll soon see, there's a lot of cake beneath Oz's icing. In fact, we think there are a dozen great lessons that will serve you well. So read on and learn why Dorothy is, indeed, one of the best managers ever to hit the screen; why the Scarecrow is the best kind of idea person; and why Glinda the Good Witch is the best kind of CEO a manager could have.

A DOZEN GREAT LESSONS FROM *THE WIZARD OF OZ*

- Great listeners learn from poor communicators
- Don't be a "Don't Bother Me" boss
- Become (like the Professor) a data-sufficiency expert
- Be the "I" of the storm
- Be a Scarecrow (and everything's a no-brainer!)
- Nothing happens without a Tin Man
- Cowardly Lions often lead the charge
- Don't forget the special effects
- Get past the gatekeepers
- Learn to mentor like CEO Glinda
- The Wicked Witch is always watching
- Expect the best and you'll most likely get it

#1 GREAT LISTENERS LEARN FROM POOR COMMUNICATORS

Opening scene: Dorothy's in a dither. Her nasty neighbor, Miss Gulch, has threatened Dorothy's dog Toto. Auntie Em and Uncle Henry are too busy to listen. They know Miss Gulch is a chronic complainer; and they dismiss Dorothy and her anxiety as an overreaction, a "little girl problem," nothing worth spending time on. So Dorothy runs to the farmhands to tell her troubles. But they also are too busy to really listen. Nonetheless, they offer Dorothy words of advice. Hunk advises Dorothy to stay away from Miss Gulch's house and avoid the possibility of antagonizing her. Zeke argues for confrontation. "Give her a piece of your mind," he says. "Spit in her eye!" Dorothy views the hands as mentors, and they have just taught her that there might be more than one way to effectively handle a situation.

Dorothy's still a kid, so we can forgive her for not knowing how to communicate effectively. But Auntie Em, Uncle Henry and the farmhands have been around the block. They should know, as good managers do, that communication is a two-way process; and *when the speaker is weak, the listener must be especially strong.* When Dorothy comes back in a panic, the adults fit her behavior into a pattern and jump to conclusions. The pattern looks like this: little girl, she's upset, Miss Gulch (again), nothing new, I'm busy, this can wait. Truth be known, however, Dorothy has important news and the devil is in the details, which nobody asks about: Toto didn't just "bother" Miss Gulch, he bit her; and Miss Gulch isn't just complaining, she's gone to the sheriff, she's got a warrant, and she's threatening to go to court! (Remember? When Miss Gulch peddles up to the ranch, she tells Em and Henry that if they don't turn Toto over, she'll sue them for damages and take their farm!)

#2 DON'T BE A "DON'T BOTHER ME" BOSS

By not listening effectively, Em and Henry not only miss important information, but they also train Dorothy to not bring them any information in the future. If you want to be kept informed, you have to take time to listen.

Having been shut down for trying to tell her story, Dorothy does what most people do when the boss is too busy to listen: she keeps her head down by going off where "she won't make any trouble." Were she treated that way at your office, you can bet that would be the last time she would be volunteering any information. No way! She'd head back to her cubicle, where she'd probably not even "prairie-dog" for a few days.

Auntie Em, Uncle Henry and the farmhands genuinely love Dorothy, but for our money they should be raising ostriches, not chickens. If you want to be informed, you have to encourage people to speak up. Sometimes the information won't be worth much, but sometimes it will. In either case you can't afford to be a "don't bother me" boss.

#3 BECOME (LIKE THE PROFESSOR)
A DATA-SUFFICIENCY EXPERT

Professor Marvel (a.k.a. The Gatekeeper, a.k.a. The Guard, a.k.a. The Wizard) would have passed his GMAT test with flying colors. If you've taken the GMAT, you'll recall the data-sufficiency section (and probably not fondly). If you haven't taken the GMAT, here's what data sufficiency is about: you're presented with a problem in math or logic and given three pieces of information that can help you solve the problem. Then you are asked not for the solution, but whether the information you were given was: A) not enough to find the solution; B) just enough to find the solution; or C) more than you needed to find the solution. It's a very tough test partly because it's structured differently from the other sections of the exam; partly because most high schools and colleges focus on getting the right answer, not getting it most efficiently; and partly because you have to remember a lot of geometric formulas you won't have used since high school and will never use again. Nonetheless, the Data Sufficiency Test is there for a good reason: gathering information takes time and money. If you gather more than you need, you're wasting time and money. Wasting time and money is antithetical to efficient business practice—hence, the data-sufficiency section on the GMAT.

Professor Marvel has an intuitive understanding of data sufficiency. Dorothy shows up at his campsite. She has a bag of food and her dog with her. She looks tired; she's hungry; she's out in the middle of nowhere by herself. Professor Marvel doesn't need to do a focus group to determine her needs. He "guesses" it all: she's running away from home because she's misunderstood there. Amazed at his deep knowledge of her situation, Dorothy decides the Professor is a wise man, so she asks his advice (Dorothy will ask ANYBODY for advice!). His intuitive knowledge fails him, so he cuts to the chase. He consults his crystal ball. While he draws it out, he asks Dorothy to close her eyes, then searches her basket for additional data that will help him help her. (That's about as efficient as one can get!) He finds a picture of a woman (Auntie Em) standing by the gate of a picket fence. It's enough, of course. When Dorothy opens her eyes, the Professor gazes into the ball saying, "I see a woman standing beside a fence." Dorothy says the woman must be Auntie Em. The Professor, armed with this new nugget of information, applies it quickly and tells Dorothy that, yes, the woman's name "is Emily." This further impresses the highly-impressionable Dorothy. Professor Marvel notes that the woman looks sad, lonely, perhaps hurt because she's missing someone—and Dorothy, of course, spills the beans on running away and then decides, guided by the Professor, to return home.

The Professor has done his good deed for the day and he hasn't wasted a fact, a word, a dollar. He has achieved maximum results from minimum research effort. When you master data sufficiency, you'll be able to do that, too.

#4 BE THE "I" OF THE STORM

There you are—in a good position with an established company and then—blam!—you're swept up in turmoil. No telling what cubicle you'll land in. You might even wind up at another company in a different town, maybe even in Oz. You're swept up in the corporate equivalent of a Level 5 twister if ever, there ever, a twister was. No matter how weird it gets, you have to position yourself in the eye of the storm, protecting yourself from the chaos around you. You can create your own eye. Your skills, self-confidence, observational skills and presence of mind can *make you* the "I" of the storm—the person who stays cool in a crisis. It works for Dorothy. Her reaction when she finds herself caught up in the tornado is not so much fear as wonder. She keeps her head, going to the window to see what's happening. When you're caught up in a storm at the office, do as Dorothy does: keep your head, gather information, watch the skies.

#5 BE A SCARECROW
(AND EVERYTHING'S A NO-BRAINER!)

If there's a recurring theme in *The Wizard of Oz*, it's that the major characters believe they lack the very traits they most possess. The Scarecrow *thinks* he lacks brains. (Clearly, if he can *think* he lacks brains, he must have some.) Not only does he have a brain, but he is always using it—and in a variety of ways. Sometimes he's reflective. For example, when Dorothy asks him how he can talk if he hasn't got a brain, he tells her he doesn't know, then adds, "some people without brains do an awful lot of talking, don't they?" Later he shows that he knows what management is supposed to be about when he asks Dorothy if he can join her on her trip to Oz, promising that "he won't try to manage things, because he can't think." If only all managers realized that thinking is the essence of their work!

When he's not sharing his astute observations, the Scarecrow applies his brain to tactics. There's that scene in the woods: Dorothy and Scarecrow are hungry and stop to pick some apples. But the apple trees aren't willing to give up their fruit and order the twosome to stop picking. Scarecrow taunts the trees. He gets them so upset they start throwing their apples at him and Dorothy. They gather the apples up and head down the road. Using his brain, the Scarecrow has tricked the trees into giving him exactly what he wanted—and exactly what they most wanted to hold onto.

In addition to being a reflective and tactical thinker, the Scarecrow is a strategic thinker. He's the one who puts together the plan to rescue Dorothy from the castle of the Wicked Witch—and it works.

Like the Scarecrow, you have a brain—and it's probably better than you think. Of course, it needs exercise. We've put together a list of ten quick brain-stretcher exercises you can do on a regular basis to keep your brain in top working order.

Ten Great Ways to Exercise Your Mind

1. **Take up a new mental pursuit at least once a year. Learn a foreign language.** Take up bird-watching. Master a video game. If you play chess, try the oriental game Go. If you play poker, try bridge or chess. Whatever it is, work at it.

2. **Move up a level in your normal pursuits.** Many people work the daily crossword puzzles in their newspapers long after they've become easy. If you're still having trouble getting through the puzzle, stick with it; but if it's become a piece of cake, it's time to find a new puzzle. If you are easily completing most standard-style crosswords, take up diagramless or cryptic crosswords. Whatever your daily pursuit, if it's becoming too easy, it's time to move up a notch. Stretch that brain!

3. **Take a different route to work every day, even if you only vary your routine by a few blocks.** Changing your path gives you a chance to observe new things. Observation gives birth to thought; habit is its death.

4. **Don't just read, read something different.** Make sure that at least 40 percent of the books you read are non-fiction books unrelated to your business. Seek out books on popular science, history and biography. If you never read science fiction, force yourself to try some—same with a mystery or two; and make time to re-read at least one book you liked when you read it in college. Rethinking is as important as thinking—maybe more important.

5. **Build your memory.** Force yourself to learn a list of something: Presidents of the United States in order; capitals of African nations; the value of *pi* to the 50th place; the first lines of Shakespeare's plays; the first sentences of Dickens' novels; the birthdays of all your direct reports. Sure, you could look these things up, but memory works your brain. Once you've got one list down, challenge yourself with another.

6. **Write your autobiography.** Or consider writing a history of your company or a brief biography of someone you admire. William Zinsser, an expert on writing, believes that writing helps us think. It makes us organize our thoughts and determine what we really know and believe. Write to think!

7. **Practice speed math.** Face it, you are impressed when someone who's just heard the same series of numbers you've heard immediately announces that their cumulative effect will be, say, a 60 percent improvement in revenues. She does this while you're still putting the numbers into your H-P Business Consultant. Your head for numbers is better than you think, but you have to exercise it; and you'll have to learn the basic tricks of speed math. Your library is full of books on how to do it.

8. **Cultivate people who ask "smart" stupid questions.** If you have kids, you've already got them close by. Kids ask questions and require explanations that force you to get into the details of things. Why is the day divided into 24 hours? Why do currents flow one direction in the northern half of the globe and the opposite direction in the southern half? Why

do we need profit? The main questions and the follow-ups can quickly send you back to the books to seek better ways to explain things. Answering "dumb" questions will make you smarter.

9. **Switch hands.** If you're left-handed, try doing things with your right hand. If you're right-handed, try doing things with your left. You probably are familiar with all of that "right-brain/left-brain" stuff so you know that the right side of the brain generally controls the left side of the body and vice versa. You also know that the right brain is credited with creative processes. We know one person who, when he is in a brainstorming session, always holds his pencil in his left hand, makes a point of rotating his left foot and makes other movements designed to work the left side of his body in order to stimulate the right side of his brain. In budget meetings, he favors the right side of his body, to stimulate the "logic" of his left brain. He says it helps him match his thinking style to the needs of the discussion.

10. **Keep notes or a diary of things that capture your attention.** If you're reading a book and like a quotation in it, don't just dog-ear the page, write it down. If you see a painting you like, make a note of who painted it, its medium, when it was painted and where you saw it. Like that wine? Make a note of it. When you write these things down, you further embed them in your memory.

Special Note: Remember your body. Your mind functions best when your body functions best. Get enough sleep and don't forget physical exercise.

#6 NOTHING HAPPENS WITHOUT A TIN MAN

The Tin Man *thinks* he needs a heart. Of course, the fact that he *cares* about having no heart, shows that he, in fact, has one. The Tin Man isn't heartless as in "cruel"; he is heartless in the sense of "lacking will." He has trouble getting his blood (or oil, if you will) pumping in the morning. Rust is only one thing that makes him lackluster; he just "doesn't have the heart" for doing things anymore. When Dorothy and the Scarecrow invite him to join them and to ask the Wizard for a heart, the Tin Man can only question the payback. "What," he asks, "if the Wizard wouldn't give me one?" By anticipating the possibility of failure, the Tin Man has managed to stay more than a little rusty. Whenever you encounter someone in your work place who asks the question, "What if it doesn't work?", you've found a Tin Man waiting to be oiled.

The Tin Man is, of course, the most caring character in the movie. The only reason he gets rusty is *because* he cares—and frets—about everything to the point of shedding tears which, when shed, cause him to rust.

In the scene prior to Dorothy's rescue, the Scarecrow comes up with the plan, but only because the Tin Man, moved to tears of concern, says "we have to do something." Even the best brains can be lazy and even the most courageous people can lack will. The prime movement in any organization comes because somebody gives a damn. In *The Wizard of Oz*, it's the Tin Man. Who are the Tin Men in your organization? The ones whose hearts are in the job (even if they think they don't have hearts and even if they don't know their hearts are still in their jobs)? If you don't have any Tin Men, your Scarecrows probably aren't thinking about the right things and the bravery of your Lions probably isn't being tested.

#7 COWARDLY LIONS OFTEN LEAD THE CHARGE

He blusters and poses; he's a big talker who puts up a good front—until Dorothy whacks him on the nose. Then we see the Lion for what he thinks he is: a 'fraidy cat or, as he describes himself in his first song, a "dandy lion." But the lion doesn't understand that while it's often okay to be afraid, it is almost never right to let fear stop you from taking the necessary action. In the opening scenes of the movie we find the Lion's human counterpart, farmhand Zeke, telling Dorothy she has to stand up to Miss Gulch and "spit in her eye." Then Dorothy falls into the pigpen where she's likely to be trampled and bitten by the hogs. Zeke doesn't stop to think—he dives into the pen and rescues her. But when he brings her out, he's visibly shaken, trembling with fear about what might have happened and realizing that he, too, could have fallen victim to the rampaging pigs. The other farmhands tease him about being afraid. Fact is, Zeke was the only one brave enough to jump into the sty. A similar thing happens when the three rescuers assault the castle: the Tin Man urges action; the Scarecrow comes up with a plan; but it's the Lion who leads the way.

#8 DON'T FORGET THE SPECIAL EFFECTS

The Wizard is a humbug, but he humbugs well. His "office" exudes authority and power. Who can doubt, in that setting, with the Wizard's over-sized head floating in space, that this character knows all and can do anything? Ideally, you are not a humbug and really know your stuff. But that's no reason to show up at meetings without wearing your best business outfit and making your presentation as exciting, clear and well-organized as possible. *How* you present is often as important as *what* you present.

Special Effects: Eleven Keys to Great Speeches and Presentations

1. **Follow Aristotle.** The art of rhetoric has advanced a lot since Aristotle's time, but most of the new stuff is purely academic. Aristotle wrote a manual, *The Rhetoric*, that has served generations of speakers well, particularly in terms of organizing presentations. Each presentation, he argued, has a beginning, a middle and an end. The best way to start is by telling your audience what you are going to cover ("tell 'em what you're going to tell 'em"). The middle is the heart of the matter and conveys your message and the reasons behind it (this is *where* you "tell 'em"). The end reiterates what you said and, if appropriate, urges action in response to your message ("tell 'em what you told 'em" and ask for the order).

2. **Don't let your appearance or behavior get in the way of your message.** Be clean, dress appropriately for your audience (better to be overdressed than underdressed), polish those shoes, and make sure your hair's combed. Sounds basic, but it's surprising how often we have heard a good speaker make a great presentation and then overheard folks in the lobby chuckling about the spot on his tie. Of course, it shouldn't matter, but it does.

3. **Show up on time.** Nobel Prize-winning author Sinclair Lewis once described an ideal speaker as anyone "who showed up ten minutes early and sober." 'Nuf said. When you show up late, you wind up in apologetic mode and that impedes your ability to

get fired up. The audience and program chairman have already started focusing on whether you'll arrive instead of how great your remarks will be. Showing up at least ten minutes early also gives you a chance to adjust to the room, to make sure your equipment is properly set up, and to answer any last-minute questions from the person who will introduce you.

4. **Never count on visual aids.** More than one presentation has been spoiled because the speaker's slides got spilled or mangled, or because a computer connection failed, a projector bulb blew, or a computer wouldn't power up. We've seen American speakers arrive in foreign countries with VHS tapes, only to find the country has no VHS players. Always have a back-up plan if your visual aids fail. Sometimes presentations are canceled on the spot because the speaker was planning to ad lib around the notes on her lost/damaged slides. Have printed copies of your slides with you, as well as a set of transparencies for use with overhead projectors.

5. **Use humor sparingly and appropriately.** One person's humor is another person's *faux pas*. Humor is especially dangerous in international speaking where your favorite joke may not make sense, may be mistranslated, or may lose its timing-dependent impact due to delays in translation. One of the most frightening moments in international speaking comes when you tell a joke, hit the punch line and look befuddled when the audience doesn't laugh. A moment later, just as you are starting to resume

your speech, the translation is completed and you are interrupted by delayed laughter from the audience! This "laugh gap" is always a problem in sequential translation, where you speak and then wait for the translation; but even simultaneous interpretation can wreck your timing. Best bet: avoid humor when abroad and use it sparingly when you're stateside.

6. **Keep within your allotted time.** Don't overstay your welcome. If you've agreed to speak for 20 minutes, don't speak for more than that. There's only one way to do this. Practice and time your speech until you've edited it to fit the allotted time. Don't expect an audience to understand that you are rambling on because you didn't respect their time enough to go over your remarks in advance. It's rude and it's a killer for your speaking career.

7. **Keep slides simple.** A good slide is like a good billboard: it features a great graphic and has fewer than ten words. If you're doing a series of thoughts, display them in sequence, adding and highlighting a line at a time as you "build" the series. Keep each line short and to the point.

8. **Have a strong close.** Always write out the last three sentences of your presentation and commit them to memory. Great presentations are often destroyed when the speaker's thoughts trail off and end in a weak "thank you." Close with a bang! (By the way, it's okay to say "thank you," but your close needs to first bring things home in a way that invites applause.) Never leave the audience wondering if

you are finished. Writing out your close in advance makes sure you *have* a close.

9. **Project energy.** If you seem tired or bored, your audience will be, too. Speakers use a variety of techniques to pump themselves up before a presentation. One speaker we know listens to a favorite Vivaldi tape. When appropriate, she asks that it be played as background music at luncheons before she takes the podium. Another insists upon taking a vigorous 15–minute walk just before meeting the audience. Another excuses himself from the podium for five minutes just before he's introduced. (He implies that he's going to the restroom, but he actually finds a quiet corner in a lobby and gives himself a pep talk!) Another speaker parks a picture of his beloved wife on the podium next to his notes and speaks to please her, his best critic. These or other techniques may work for you. Whatever you do, don't be boring. Speak as if you give a damn!

10. **It's better to read than to ramble.** If you're not a professional speaker, it's okay to read your speech (as long as you're not reading it for the first time). Reading a speech has several advantages: first, if you can read it, it means you (or someone) had to write it. Consequently, the speech can be structured and timed. Second, if you're reading the speech, you have a record of what you said. Third, if you're reading a speech, you are less likely to flub a quotation or a number. There are, of course, pitfalls to reading speeches. You can't just sight read. You need to read through your remarks a couple of times before you deliver them. That will enable you to look

up from your remarks occasionally and maintain eye contact with the audience. It also means the audience will know you've read it before and thought about what you were going to say. That's a sign of respect and audiences like it.

11. **Collect examples of great speeches from the movies.** The movies in this series of books are filled with examples of great motivational speeches. Watch the awards scene in *The Wizard of Oz*. Pay attention to how the Wizard presents the diploma, watch and medal. Listen to the way he structures the presentation. Watch *Executive Suite* and note how Donald Walling secures the presidency of Tredway company with a speech that would do any CEO proud. Listen to Coach Dale outline his thoughts on how teams work in *Hoosiers*. Listen to Sigourney Weaver explain her work rules to Tess McGill in *Working Girl*. These are just a few examples from movies that can help you be a more articulate speaker.

#9 GET PAST THE GATEKEEPERS

At the gates of Oz, Dorothy and her friends meet the Gate-keeper, a pettifogging bureaucratic nebbish. First, he chastises the quartet for failing to read a sign he has forgotten to post. Then, when Dorothy and her friends ask to see the Wizard, he tells them "nobody can see the Great Oz" and expects them to go away. Dorothy says she *must* see the Wizard and cites her authority (she tells him she's been sent by Glinda and she wears the red slippers to prove it).

But the Gatekeeper doesn't open the door. Then the Wicked Witch flies over and sky-writes a request that Dorothy be turned over to her. The Gatekeeper wonders who the witch wants and Dorothy tells him her name. "The Witch's Dorothy," he says. "That's different." But it's really not and he still won't let her in. Neither the Good Witch's authority nor Dorothy's own notoriety has worked. In frustration, Dorothy breaks into tears, sobbing about how she'll never get back to the farm and to her Uncle Henry and Auntie Em. Hearing her sobs, the Gatekeeper admits Dorothy, wiping tears from his own eyes and noting that he "had an Auntie Em himself once."

Getting past gatekeepers is an art and Dorothy's pretty good at it. She opens the gate by being persistent and by trying several approaches.

Gatekeepers are everywhere and they are there for a reason. Busy, successful people don't have time to waste. Gatekeepers are paid to keep time wasters away. Be sure if you do get around them, that you'll be worth spending time with. Otherwise, both you and the gatekeeper will find yourselves outside the door.

#10 LEARN TO MENTOR LIKE CEO GLINDA

Consider the geo-politics of Oz. It's a world of contrast and conflict. There are pleasant, well-run countries in the North and South, presided over by benevolent queens (okay, good witches). The Munchkins live just within their borders, singing, dancing and frolicking beside the Yellow Brick Road. Then there are the Witchdoms of the East and West, ruled by evil sisters controlling armies of ape-like beings held in thrall. The Munchkins are caught up in a border war involving Glinda, the Good Witch of the North, and the surviving Wicked Witch of the West.

Glinda needs to protect her borders and her Munchkins and, good as her magic wand is, she needs help if she's to overcome the Wicked Witch, establish a New World Order, and free herself from having to intervene personally in every little crisis. She's been there, done that and she isn't getting any younger. Time to delegate. But to whom? Fortunately, Dorothy drops in just in time—and in just the right place—to be a real help, assuming, of course, that Dorothy's not a witch, too. (Glinda's been in a two-witch war; she doesn't need any new opponents.) Glinda also knows that her allies must be capable and that Dorothy has a lot to learn.

Glinda, noting that Dorothy has killed the Witch of the East and made an enemy of the Witch of the West, advises the girl to leave Oz. But, says Glinda, she doesn't know how Dorothy can do that. Glinda is telling a little white lie here. She knows the secret to leaving, but she's not telling because she needs Dorothy to go to Oz. She needs help from both Dorothy and the Wizard if she is to rid Oz of the remaining Wicked Witch.

Glinda will get what she wants, but Dorothy will also grow as a result, learning valuable lessons. Glinda will take credit for being a great teacher—and it's not undeserved. The first lesson she teaches is one of delegation. She tells Dorothy the Wizard might be able to help her get home, but that the journey to Oz is a long one. Dorothy needs more data and asks for it (she's very good at asking). Glinda tells her to follow the Yellow Brick Road, that the Munchkins will help her get started, and that she should never take the ruby slippers off her feet. Dorothy seeks more information, but Glinda is a master delegator: she waves her wand and disappears! Remind you of any managers you've worked for?

> ## GLINDA T. GOOD , CEO
> ### Managerial Affirmations
>
> - Cheerfully welcome all new Dorothys.
> - Defend your turf. (Bad witches not allowed!)
> - Suggest, don't tell.
> - Provide adequate support (enough Munchkins).
> - Empowerment means "get out of their way." (Wave wand and disappear!)
> - Don't micromanage. If you must intervene, be invisible.
> - Don't do, teach!
> - Show up at the end and praise everyone.
> - Make sure they know YOU taught them.

The more we learn about Glinda, the more we see how effective she is in getting what she wants by helping her aides learn. Despite the fact that they don't see Glinda, she's clearly behind the scenes keeping watch. We learn this in the scene in which Glinda sends snow to counteract the effects of the sleep-inducing poppies. Glinda never rushes in dramatically to fix everything herself and, in the process, undermine Dorothy's self-confidence as a manager. Even when Glinda reappears at the end of the movie, it is only to make sure that Dorothy has learned the lessons of the ruby slippers for herself.

#11 THE WICKED WITCH IS ALWAYS WATCHING

Your competition may not have a crystal ball but, like the Wicked Witch of the West, they have an eye out for what you're doing—and it pays to keep an eye on them as well. Throughout the movie, the Wicked Witch knows where Dorothy is, what Dorothy is doing and can assess the prospects for Dorothy's success. When she sees Dorothy making progress, she throws up obstacles. ("Poppies! Poppies will put them to sleep!")

Short of illegal wiretaps (if crystal balls *really* worked, they'd be outlawed, too), how do you keep tabs on your competitors? Sure, it's easy to read annual reports, but they only tell you where the company's been, not necessarily what it's up to now. You can pump vendors, former employees and customers for information, too; but that's a dangerous game. These sources often supply good information, but they can be channels of misinformation and disinformation as well. In developing your own crystal ball you must first ask yourself what you really need to know. Gossip about a competitor may be interesting, but is it really useful? Ask yourself, "If I know this, what will I do?" If you don't know what you'd do with a piece of information, don't seek it out; it will only distract you. And since the Wicked Witch—your competitor—is always watching, you need to think of the information you would least like him or her to have and make sure you have the mechanisms in place to give it maximum protection from leaks, squeaks and sneak-thieves.

#12 EXPECT THE BEST AND YOU'LL MOST LIKELY GET IT

The Wizard's ultimate secret is summed up in a lyric: "I never did give nothin' to the Tin Man that he didn't already have." The Tin Man has a heart; he just thinks he doesn't. The Lion is courageous, but thinks he's a coward. The Scarecrow is a genius, but thinks he's a dolt. Shakespeare once said, "There is nothing either good or bad; but thinking makes it so." Management wizards get the most from their staffs by helping staff members better use the brains, passion and courage they already have. Wizards do this by helping people see themselves as able, by praising success, by helping them visualize themselves in new ways. Remember when the Scarecrow gets his diploma? Now he thinks of himself as smart. Knowledge he has been suppressing comes spewing forth! If you want smart people, expect them to be smart. If you want brave people, set expectations of bravery; and if you want people to be passionate in their work, to have heart, start with the assumption that they *are* committed. You'll be surprised how often people will respond to the expectations you have of them. You might even start seeing yourself as a wizard!

DISCUSSION QUESTIONS

1. Who is your favorite character in this movie and why? Are you like that character? Do you want to be? Why?
2. Dorothy builds an effective team out of three characters who think they have no brain, no guts and no heart. Are there people on your team who do not appreciate their own strengths? Has watching and reviewing *The Wizard of Oz* given you any ideas about how you can help them build self-confidence and maximize their performance?
3. Imagine your company as Oz—a place where you've had an interesting time but are now ready to leave. What is the Kansas of your dreams? Does it really still exist? Can you get there from here?

4. What are your "ruby slippers?" What are the things you have readily at hand that, if used properly, will take you where you want to go?

5. Dorothy receives a big sendoff from the Munchkins prior to her journey to The Emerald City. The Munchkins think she's special and know her mission is important, so they trot out the Lullaby League, the Lollipop Guild and the Mayor. When you send people off on major assignments, do you make them feel special? What might you do? What are the pros and cons of doing it?

THE BRIDGE ON THE RIVER KWAI:

Going to the Dogs
by Going by the Book

Nicholson (Alec Guinness) and Saito (Sessue Hayakawa) match wills over roast beef and Scotch. *Photo credit: Photofest.*

WATCH AND READ IF:

- You have difficulty dealing with ambiguity.

- You never question rules and need every rule spelled out.

- You have difficulty with cross-cultural issues.

- People tell you that you're not a good listener or suffer from "blind spots."

- You have difficulty linking daily activities to corporate mission.

THE BRIDGE ON THE RIVER KWAI:

Going to the Dogs
by Going by the Book

As part of a corporate exchange program, you and a team of American engineers have been loaned to an Asian firm for a year, while a team from that company works in your place. You're not sure why your company has participated in the exchange, particularly since the host firm competes with your company in several key international markets. Your bosses back home haven't asked you to spy for them—in fact, all they've said is that you should get along and do what you're told.

From Day One, the assignment proves rocky. The corporate culture at the new place is very different from the one you're used to back home. Here, for example, engineers don't have offices and they are expected to pitch in on production as well as design. Everyone, it seems, is expected to do everything. The host company's top manager is a stickler about this. When you tell him that's not the kind of duty you and your crew signed up for, he assigns the lot of you to janitorial duty for a week. You and your colleagues are ready to quit on the spot, but don't because there might be repercussions back home that could jeopardize your careers. You do, however, stick to your guns; and eventually the top manager backs down on janitorial duty. He had no choice

THE BRIDGE ON THE RIVER KWAI

UK (1957): War

161 minutes. Color. Available
on videocassette and laserdisc.

Audience Rating: **NR**

CAST LIST

<u>Performer</u>	<u>Character</u>
William Holden	Shears
Alec Guinness	Col. Nicholson
Jack Hawkins	Maj. Warden
Sessue Hayakawa	Col. Saito
James Donald	Maj. Clipton
Geoffrey Horne	Lt. Joyce
Andre Morell	Col. Green
Peter Williams	Capt. Reeves
John Boxer	Maj. Hughes
Percy Herbert	Grogan
Harold Goodwin	Baker
Ann Sears	Nurse
Henry Okawa	Capt. Kanematsu
K. Katsumoto	Lt. Miura
M.R.B. Chakrabandhu	Yai
Vilaiwan Seeboonreaung	
Ngamta Suphaphongs	
Javanart Punynchoti	
Kannikar Wowklee	Siamese Girls

Produced by Sam Spiegel
Directed by David Lean
Written by Pierre Boulle, Michael Wilson and Carl Foreman
Based on the novel by Pierre Boulle

in the matter: the plant's chief project is falling increasingly behind schedule. He knows only you and your team can help get it back on track.

Your crew thinks you're a hero because you've backed the plant manager down. You, however, don't think he has backed down far enough. In your mind, he needs a lesson in humility. You decide the best way to hand him one is by showing him what a group of American engineers can do when they are allowed free rein. Therefore, you tell your team to make every effort to get the project on schedule—and make product improvements while doing so. If you succeed, you will have organized the project in a way that not only keeps morale high, but also demonstrates the superiority of your company's approach to project management.

A member of your team points out that you shouldn't be helping the company you're on loan to. In fact, she says, you should be doing as little as possible to assist the project, even stalling it, while you learn everything you can about this competitor. She argues that success for the project could lead to harm for your own company.

You argue that doing poor work is just not the way your company does things. You also argue that if your team performs well enough, the competitor will be demoralized by the superiority of your skills and will likely decide not to compete with you at all.

The situation just described, although hypothetical, is similar to that faced by the prisoners of war in David Lean's 1957 classic, *The Bridge on the River Kwai*. Filled with irony and ambiguity, *Kwai* is a superb vehicle for discussing corporate mission and the disconnects that can occur when trying to achieve it. Two army colonels—one a captive British engineer, the other a rigid Japanese prison-camp commandant—match wills while attempting to carry out their orders, obey the rules of their respective military cultures,

The Story of a Real
Skills Exchange

Technical exchange agreements like the hypothetical example that begins this chapter are rare in business, but they do occur. In 1936, for example, Japan's Nissan Motors and Graham-Paige, an American automotive company, participated in such an exchange. Graham-Paige needed money; Nissan needed technology. They agreed that Nissan would be sold designs and tooling for the chassis and body of the 1937 Graham Crusader automobile, along with designs for a six-cylinder engine and a 1/2 ton truck. These designs gave Nissan the foundation for large-scale manufacturing of trucks, cars and buses. Graham got $390,000 in much-needed cash. Graham engineers helped get the project launched in Japan. Nissan learned everything it could about Graham's processes and proudly paraded the civilian version of the car around the Japanese countryside. The acquired technology was later used in the Nissan Model 80 truck—the truck of choice for the Japanese military when it invaded China in 1938. By 1942, the technology was being employed against American and Allied troops fighting in the Pacific Theater of World War II.

preserve their self-respect and, not least, build a bridge. While Colonels Saito and Nicholson battle each other, a British-Canadian-American commando team treks through the jungle to destroy the bridge before Japanese troop trains can cross it. Amid the chaos of war, leadership lessons dealing with mission, motivation, teamwork and chain of command abound.

Kwai won seven Oscars, including Best Actor and Best Picture, and was ranked No. 13 on The American Film Institute's list of the Top 100 motion pictures ever made. It's also one of our favorites for leadership training because it shows how leaders can fail when they allow ego, blind spots and poor judgment to stand in the way of accomplishing their missions.

Here's a quick review of the action:

The British have ordered a battalion under the command of Colonel Nicholson to surrender to the Japanese. The battalion is marched off to a prisoner-of-war labor camp under the command of Colonel Saito. The camp's prisoners are being used to build a railroad bridge over the river Kwai in Siam (now Thailand). The bridge will form a vital link in a strategic Japanese railroad linking Bangkok to Rangoon.

No sooner do the British troops arrive in camp than Nicholson and Saito face off over Nicholson's insistence that his officers not be forced to perform manual labor. He insists that they be assigned to administrative duties as required by the Geneva Convention. Saito refuses Nicholson's demands. The bridge is behind schedule and Saito believes only the use of every able-bodied man as a laborer will get it back on track. Nicholson, a stubborn commander and something of a snob, refuses to back down. Saito incarcerates the colonel along with his officers and sends the other prisoners to work. But when the bridge falls farther behind schedule, Saito backs down, rescinds the manual labor requirement and permits the bridge to be built under *British* direction. Nicholson decides to use the bridge project to demonstrate British cultural superiority. Not only will his men build the bridge, but they will shame the Japanese by building the best possible bridge and completing it on time. Despite concerns raised by his lieutenants that such a course of action borders on treason, Nicholson succeeds in getting his officers and men to comply with his wishes.

Meanwhile, Shears, an American prisoner, escapes the camp and recuperates from the ordeal of doing so at a military installation in Ceylon. There he is reluctantly recruited to join a British-American-Canadian commando team assigned to parachute into Siam and destroy the Kwai bridge. The commander of the expedition is Major Warden, a British commando. Shears will guide the team to its destination.

Nicholson and the British prisoners complete the construction of a quality bridge on time. Nicholson has preserved the morale and discipline of troops under his command, but has jeopardized the lives of thousands of Allied soldiers and the chance for Allied victory.

On the morning the first train is to cross the bridge, Nicholson spots signs of sabotage by the commando team and joins Saito in trying to prevent the bridge's destruction. In the end, Nicholson, Saito and all the commandos—except Warden—are killed. As a final irony, Nicholson, hit by a mortar fragment, falls dead upon the plunger of the commandos' detonator, blowing up the bridge just as the Japanese train approaches and sending both bridge and train into the river.

Only at the last moment before his death does Nicholson realize that his single-minded pursuit of the bridge's construction was dangerously misguided.

Kwai's plot is outstanding, but the movie's main strength is in its characterizations. In analyzing the movie from a business perspective, our principle focus will be on the personalities of Saito, Nicholson and Warden and the way they view their missions and lead their teams.

SAITO

Colonel Saito is a bully who prides himself on being a civilized man and an adherent of the ancient Japanese warrior's code, bushido. On both counts, his pride is misplaced. Nicholson characterizes him as the "worst commanding officer I've ever met." Saito is charged with completing the bridge on time at all costs. He is an experienced officer and has a team of Japanese engineers under his command—but he has too few Japanese soldiers to construct the bridge, so he must build it with prisoners of war. Conditions in the prison camp are deplorable. When Nicholson's battalion arrives, they find prisoners dying of disease and overwork. In Saito's view the prisoners are expendable: Japanese victories will provide replacement workers, meaning that he can literally afford to work prisoners to death. He brooks no opposition and the camp is located so that escape—although frequently attempted— is impossible.

Saito is not only a poor manager of people, but also of his project. The bridge falls increasingly behind schedule. While this is partially due to British sabotage, the real problem lies with the structure's location: the Japanese have chosen a site where the river's bottom is too soft to support the bridge. Although Saito's engineers must know this, they also know that questioning Saito's decisions—particularly, if it causes him embarrassment—is a fundamental violation of bushido. Under that code, the river must be spanned *and* personal honor must also be served. The double-bind created by Saito's obsession with bushido's unwritten, but controlling, concepts literally keeps Saito from finding the firm foundation on which to build the bridge.

Throughout the film, Saito violates bushido's fundamental tenet: self-control. He frequently shows anger; he cries; he is morose; and, clearly, he is *never* happy in his work! Saito's lack of self-control makes him inconsistent both as a manager and as a negotiator. He stakes out strong positions, then backs down from them. For example, he threatens to shoot the officers, but doesn't. He punishes Nicholson, then relents. He shorts the prisoners' rations, then gives them "presents." In all cases, Saito's actions demonstrate his weakness and desperation. His continual efforts to dictate solutions only underscore his lack of real control over the circumstances in which he finds himself. As camp commandant, he has only the authority of rank, which is always a poor substitute for the authority of substance and volunteered respect—the type of respect accorded true samurai.

Self-control is not Saito's only violation of the code he espouses. He is self-focused and unfair (not only to the British but to his own officers, one of whom he uses as a scapegoat for the bridge's problems). He shows weakness in his actions and is somewhat effete. When we first see him, he is sitting in his well-appointed quarters dressed in ceremonial robes. Later we learn of his fondness for imported Scotch, which he prefers to his native saki. Unlike true samurai who scorned formal education, Saito has an academic background: he was an art student and spent three years of study in London. He also was a reluctant soldier (having been forced to enter the army by his father's insistence). A true samurai would likely consider

Saito brutish, over-schooled, self-pampering and unworthy of samurai status.

Instead of grasping and practicing the basic concepts of bushido, Saito focuses only on efforts to save face. When he talks about the need to complete the bridge, it is never in terms of its importance to the Japanese military effort, but only in terms of what failure will mean to his own career. His attempts to save face force him to seek compromise. In one series of decisions, he progressively offers to relieve first Nicholson, then all senior officers, and finally all officers of manual labor. He creates a pretext—celebration of the Japanese victory over Russia in 1905—as a face-saving excuse to offer a general amnesty.

Saito has other problems as a manager. He does not, for example, delegate well, preferring to micromanage. When he removes Lt. Miura from command of the bridge project, he appoints himself to the post, taking on the details of day-to-day management—and doing an even worse job than Miura had been doing.

NICHOLSON

Nicholson is a terrible manager, too—and for many of the same reasons as Saito. At first, both we and his subordinates are blinded to the colonel's flaws by our admiration for his epic heroism in standing up for principle against Saito's brutishness. But even as we admire him, we begin to realize that Nicholson is a bit of a stuffed shirt. (It may not have been intentional, but the film's costumers seem to have actually stuffed Alec Guinness' shirt so that his chest puffs out like a pouter pigeon's!)

Nicholson also has a fondness for parsing fine points of

law and military behavior. We see this when he suggests that, having been ordered to surrender, any attempts at escape "might be a violation of military law." He is also a stickler for form. When he leads his conquered troops into the prison yard, it is as if they are going to an audience with the Queen. He demands precision marching, clear and prompt response to commands, proper formation, chins up. If Saito is governed by his warped view of an unwritten code, Nicholson is ruled by an inflexible sense of British honor and the letter of military law. He is, of course, both correct and admirable in his stubborn insistence that officers not be required to do manual labor. But this same inflexibility, along with his rejection of good advice from his subordinates and his extraordinary determination to "go by the book," leads him to substitute a lesser good (maintaining troop order and morale) for a greater one (aiding the British war effort by giving the Japanese as little support as possible).

Nicholson's actions confound his officers, particularly Clipton who questions his commander's plan, noting that building a good bridge could be considered an act of treason. Nicholson, of course, dismisses the suggestion with close reasoning (watch out for those close reasoners—they can find a justification for anything!). He tells Clipton it is not treasonous to maintain order, preserve the troops' sense of dignity, and teach the Japanese a lesson in British values. He tells Clipton, in a patronizing manner that will brook no further argument, that "while you are a good doctor, you have a lot to learn about command."

No doubt you've faced such a manager yourself: one whose sense of himself as a great leader and moral guardian enables him to pull not only rank, but also experience on you—one who will not consider anything you have to say. Such managers leave you feeling that you are, no matter how talented, a lesser being!

Once the bridge has been built, Nicholson continues to self-justify his actions, noting that the Japanese train will carry British sick and wounded to better hospital facilities—totally ignoring that the train's primary purpose will be to carry Japanese supplies and men to battles in which Allied lives will be endangered!

WARDEN

Now here's a man who knows his mission. He also knows what kind of team he needs and how to get the right people for the team. (If he can appeal to the cynical and disillusioned Shears, he's a master.) Warden demonstrates the will to overcome adverse circumstances and see his mission accomplished. He is a great manager and his mastery provides an important counterpoint to the failures of Saito and Nicholson.

Warden knows when to obey the rules and when to toss them out (watch how he blackmails Shears into joining the team!).

Warden seems to have a good boss himself in Colonel Green, but we don't see enough of Green to know for sure. We do know that, in his brief scenes, Green (like Warden) asks those under him for advice and suggests rather than orders actions—something Saito would never, and Nicholson seldom, do. A perfect example of this comes when Green seeks input on Lt. Joyce's qualifications for the commando mission: he asks the members of the team to decide whether Joyce should join them.

> ### Saito and Nicholson: A Two-Headed Coin
>
> Despite minor differences, Saito and Nicholson are remarkably similar. It takes a while to realize this because, in the film's early moments, we are tricked into seeing Saito as a lawbreaker (flouting the Geneva Convention) and Nicholson as a principled hero. (The trick is easy to pull off because *Kwai's* English-speaking audiences had become accustomed, in the early post-war period, to seeing war movies in which the Japanese were propagandized as "the bad guys.")
>
> Our first impressions change, however, as the story unfolds. Both colonels turn out to be stubborn egoists; both are snobbish and affected (think of Saito and his penchant for fine imported Scotch!); each is certain of his culture's superiority. The two colonels believe in their respective codes of honor and are convinced that it is important to stay true to those codes and their military traditions. Both are intelligent, well-educated and experienced officers. The fact that they are of equal rank is a signal that they share many other traits.

Among the lessons of *The Bridge on the River Kwai*:

#1 OBSERVE CAREFULLY
AND WATCH THOSE BLIND SPOTS

A blind spot is a prejudice that one has but is usually unaware of. Pre-conceptions about persons and situations often lead to mistaken analysis which, in turn, leads to misjudgment. Blind spots are usually caused by a lack of empathic power—by the inability to see a situation from

10 LEADERSHIP LESSONS FROM THE BRIDGE ON THE RIVER KWAI

- Observe carefully and watch those blind spots
- Today's victory can be a stepping stone to tomorrow's defeat
- Never let them see you sweat!
- Keep the greater good top of mind
- Always ask "Why?"
- Focus on "win-win" solutions
- Maintain perspective
- No amount of loyalty makes up for stupidity!
- A leader's major flaws are often masked by minor strengths
- Practice what you preach (no bush-league bushido, please!)

different points of view, particularly the point of view of an opponent. In today's world of diverse workforces, *understanding how to understand* becomes more important than ever. Leaders must learn to view situations from different perspectives and postpone conclusions until multiple observations have been made and confirmed by others.

#2 TODAY'S VICTORY CAN BE A STEPPING STONE TO TOMORROW'S DEFEAT

It's an old lesson dating back to ancient Greece. The phrase "pyrrhic victory" applies to situations in which winning a battle means losing the war. Nicholson's victory on a fine point of law makes him a hero, but ultimately leads him to folly and death.

#3 NEVER LET THEM SEE YOU SWEAT!

Did you notice how cool Saito looks when the prisoners first enter the camp? He's been relaxing in his robes in his well-appointed quarters. A servant operates a manually-controlled fan that keeps the colonel's rooms as cool as possible. Saito moves slowly and deliberately as he puts on his uniform, then steps outside to greet the new British prisoners. His uniform is crisp and, though he stands unshaded under the midday sun, he doesn't break even a bead of sweat. His coolness enhances the sense that he is truly in command of himself and the camp. We soon learn, however, that Saito's ability to keep cool physically is not matched by emotional coolness. Each time Saito confronts Nicholson, it is the British colonel who keeps his emotional cool intact—and wins his point. The lesson is simple: in situations involving confrontation and negotiation, your power is enhanced by keeping your emotions in place—in keeping your cool.

#4 KEEP THE GREATER GOOD TOP OF MIND

The world of management is full of ambiguity. If correct decisions could be codified, no one would ever have to exercise judgment—yet judgment is the essence of leadership.

Both Saito and Nicholson routinely worry over the small stuff and let their quests for egoistic victories get in the way of accomplishing the big stuff: building the bridge and helping the British war efforts, respectively. This is a hallmark of poor managers. They do well at tasks—sometimes the wrong tasks—because they cannot or will not think strategically. While Saito achieves his end—the Kwai bridge is built well and on time—he wastes time and effort and loses face. Had Saito gotten his priorities correctly ordered from the get-go, he might well have been able to build the bridge, control the prisoners and save face, too.

Training in specifics is never a substitute for training in judgment. Large organizations usually rely on the expediency of formal training to assimilate individuals into a coherent whole in which everyone knows the basic rules. Saito and Nicholson know the rules all right—Nicholson even carries them in his pocket! But just knowing the rules is not enough: you need some comprehension of what led to the rules and what outcomes the rules are supposed to insure. Over-reliance on "the book" often produces weak judgments when critical actions are needed to assure success or survival. Leaders have to consider the total picture and adjust for circumstances. Blinded by their egos, Saito and Nicholson fail to do this.

Good training focuses first on teaching specific actions to be taken in specific and normal situations. Usually, when new circumstances are encountered, lower-echelon managers are urged to consult higher ups who may have more latitude and confidence in writing a temporary order. When higher ups cannot be reached and decisions must be made, on-site managers must make the call. If they've been trained in the principles of good judgment, they'll usually make the right call. If, however, the call proves wrong, good organizations will revise their rules and training processes to assure better decisions in future, similar circumstances.

As a manager, Nicholson does the right thing in his successful attempt to enforce the Geneva Convention—there is a clear rule, applicable to his specific situation. He does the wrong thing, however, in deciding to help with the bridge. No rule governs how much or how little the British prisoners should help the Japanese. He cannot appeal to higher authority, so he has to *make the call* himself. Unfortunately, he makes the wrong call.

If you are in charge of the training and development programs at your organization, be certain to emphasize critical thinking and judgment skills. Warden easily understands when it is okay to break the rules (blackmail is, after all, a no-no) to accomplish his goals. In today's business, this is often called "thinking outside the nine dots." The phrase is derived from a puzzle you've probably faced in a training session. The mistake most people make in trying to solve the puzzle is to assume that non-existent rules govern the solution. The only way to solve the puzzle is to go beyond the preconceived rules.

#5 ALWAYS ASK "WHY?"

Why was the British battalion ordered to surrender? We aren't told, but Nicholson never questions why, he only follows orders and does it. Perhaps the order was given in hopes that Nicholson would sabotage the bridge-building project! Or in hopes that he would gather information on conditions in the camp. Nicholson seems not to have considered these possibilities. Having been ordered to surrender, he assumes only that he and his men should not attempt escape because it COULD be a violation of military law. It proves a fatal assumption. The lesson is simple: leaders must regularly ask themselves "why?" If they are cut off from the people who can tell them why, they must figure things out for themselves. Leaders do this by questioning themselves and considering all possibilities. (By the way, if you have trouble coming up with all conceivable possibilities, act like a three-year-old. As any parent can tell you, a child's constant question after any answer is "why?"

If you don't have a three-year-old around, make a point of asking yourself "why" three times during any decision-making process.)

#6 FOCUS ON "WIN-WIN" SOLUTIONS

Saito operates on the theory that "if you give me *some* of the things I want, I'll give you *some* of the things you want." The problem with compromise is that something important must be sacrificed by each side to an agreement. Compromise is invariably a "lose/lose" approach. Saito may not be happy about having to compromise, but he will do so, if necessary. Nicholson, on the other hand, is a rigidly all-or-nothing person. He will not compromise with Saito and sees their conflict only in terms of a "win-lose" outcome in which Nicholson must win his point and Saito must lose face. Of course, "win-lose" scenarios have serious downsides. In this case, Nicholson's desire to win *at any cost* leads him toward treason.

Both men would have benefited from training in the fundamentals of "win-win" solutions—the type that transcend a conflict and attempt to achieve the key desires of both sides. A "win-win" in *Kwai* might have resulted had Nicholson and Saito sat down as professionals of good will, listened carefully to one another's positions and tried to satisfy each other concerning the major issues that separated them. Saito might then have agreed to comply with the Geneva Convention if, in turn, he could count on Nicholson to obey the rules of law, end all sabotage and follow Saito's commands to the letter. If Nicholson agreed, he would have preserved troop morale, avoided punishment for himself and his officers, obeyed his orders and been true to his mission. Saito would have ended all sabotage, filled his manpower needs and preserved face. (It's a moot question whether or not the bridge would have been completed on time, but the responsibility for completion would clearly have been in Japanese hands, where it belonged.)

The "win-win" approach, of course, doesn't always work in corporate life; but it should be the starting point of any important negotiation. Had Nicholson and Saito used "win-win," they would have demonstrated real managerial skill. (They also would have left us with a rather boring movie!)

#7 MAINTAIN PERSPECTIVE

As the bridge project progresses under British command, Nicholson begins to see it as his legacy. He is intrigued by the idea that, if built with elms, it could rival the longevity of the London Bridge! We later see Nicholson posting a sign commemorating the bridge's building by British troops—an advertisement for his own misjudgment! He has made the mistake of getting so close to the project that he cannot put it in proper perspective.

#8 NO AMOUNT OF LOYALTY
MAKES UP FOR STUPIDITY!

The Japanese team is simply not competent. They have chosen the wrong site for the bridge; they have chosen the wrong tactics for motivating the work force; they do not question their own bad decisions. Saito believes the bridge can be built if more men work faster. Instead he should be re-examining (literally) the foundations of the project.

Business and Bushido:
The Warrior's Code

There is a saying in Japan: "Business is War." The statement illuminates the transformation of once and future samurai into international merchant road warriors.

The adoption of bushido by Japanese businessmen elevates business to a higher position in modern Japanese society than it had traditionally held (it was previously the lowest of the four estates). Major principles of bushido conduct include:

- Patriotism. Traditionally this meant loyalty to one's country; today it is the "be true to your school" code that attaches itself to Japanese corporations. (Great examples of this can be found by viewing the movie and using the study guide for the 1986 Michael Keaton film, *Gung Ho*—also in the **moviesforbusiness.com**™ series.)
- Sense of shame
- Self-sacrifice
- Justice
- Martial spirit
- Frugality
- Modesty
- Refined manners
- Actions, not words
- Self control (calmness of behavior, composure of mind, no crying)
- Love and benevolence, particularly toward the downtrodden

While Colonel Saito gives lip service to bushido, we leave it to you to decide if he exemplifies enough of its traits to qualify as a modern samurai.

#9 A LEADER'S MAJOR FLAWS
ARE OFTEN MASKED BY MINOR STRENGTHS

Strong technical skills often become weaknesses when used to support misguided strategy.

Nicholson is personally brave, cares about his troops, knows a thing or two about building bridges and understands the basics of maintaining military discipline. (At one point, remember, he gets Saito to agree that the duty of an officer is to command and that effective command requires that officers be treated with respect. If they are not, he says, chaos and demoralization are the inevitable result. He's right!) But Nicholson's minor strengths are not enough to overcome his greatest weakness: letting rules substitute for judgment.

#10 PRACTICE WHAT YOU PREACH
(NO BUSH-LEAGUE BUSHIDO, PLEASE!)

Saito talks a good game when it comes to bushido, but he is a terrible practitioner. A true samurai would not force sick men to work, let alone threaten to shoot unarmed men. Saito's talk of bushido rings hollow throughout and especially when he knocks British codes saying, "This is war, not a game of cricket." War is not cricket, of course, but the codes of both a samurai and the British military tradition call for adherence to rules of conduct similiar to those of a game. Nicholson, too, winds up violating the rules he has fought to have Saito put in place. Near the film's end, Nicholson orders his officers to do manual labor. (Actually, he asks them to volunteer; but as Shears has noted earlier, "When a man like your colonel suggests something, it's an order.") Nicholson also "suggests" that men recuperating in the hospital pitch in. Both actions, he argues, are mandated by "crisis," but the only crisis is that the enemy will not have use of the Kwai bridge. To order sick men and officers to work—and particularly to achieve *that* end—runs counter to the "rules of the civilized world" Nicholson has previously championed.

DISCUSSION QUESTIONS

1. Think about how Saito and Nicholson might have behaved if their roles were reversed; that is, if Saito were the head of Japanese POWs in a British camp run by Nicholson. How do you think someone like Saito would have behaved? What kind of goals would he have as the prisoners' leader?

2. Imagine Warden in Nicholson's position as a colonel of the surrendered battalion. How might he have dealt with the issue of manual labor for officers? If he, like Saito, had been in charge of the camp and the bridge project, how would he have gone about getting the bridge built?

3. Does your company have unwritten codes that are the corporate equivalent of bushido? Are the origins of these codes ever discussed formally? Do all associates understand not only what the code requires, but why?

4. Does your company's employee policy book read like a book of statutes, or does it present a thought-process with guidelines that encourage and empower good judgment in situations demanding flexibility? What are the merits of these two different approaches to policy manuals?

5. How do you feel about the "war is business" metaphor, which is not only used in Japan, but is common in other cultures? War, after all, is destructive; while business, done well, is constructive. What other differences (and similarities) exist between the world of warriors and the world of business people?

6. Think about the role of conflict in the achievement of any goal. Had Saito agreed to Nicholson's stand on manual labor when first asked, how might Nicholson and his men have viewed their work on the bridge? Would they have tried to build the best possible bridge? Do you think the bridge would have been built on time? Without the initial conflict what do think the movie would have been like?

7. The military is often cited as a good training ground for leadership, and military background is sometimes considered a plus on job applications. Why does it go so wrong with Nicholson and Saito? Is the problem with their training or their judgment?

MOBY DICK:

Captain Ahab

Throws His Mission Overboard

The obsessive Captain Ahab (Gregory Peck) prepares to harpoon his nemesis, Moby Dick. *Photo credit:* Photofest.

WATCH AND READ IF:

- You have trouble speaking up.

- You're interested in "role of the firm" issues.

- You have to design compensation plans.

- You suspect your industry is in decline.

- You like motivational and human-resource issues.

MOBY DICK:

Captain Ahab
Throws His Mission Overboard

Your boss is nuts!

He's started using company resources to achieve a personal goal. He has managed to hypnotize the whole staff (except you, of course) into following his lead. He's offered them big rewards and exacted pledges of loyalty! Why do the owners put up with this? Don't they realize how crazy he is? He's let whole projects and major chunks of business go by the wayside while he works on his own agenda. The other night you confronted him at Starbucks' over a hot latté. You told him your concerns and reminded him of his duty to the company. He took it badly and reminded you that your duty was to <u>him</u> and that stirring up trouble could cost you your job. That took the wind out of your sails! The boss may be nuts—but he <u>is</u> the boss—which means he has the power and you don't. You could go directly to the owners, but it's unlikely you'll get a hearing. You are based in the most remote company office, and at headquarters they probably have no idea who you are or what you do— even if you could get through to them.

In *Moby Dick*, Captain Ahab's obsession with capturing the white whale blinds him to his duty both to his employers

MOBY DICK

US (1956): Adventure

116 minutes. Color. Available
on videocassette and laserdisc.

Audience Rating: **NR**

CAST LIST

<u>Performer</u>	<u>Character</u>
Gregory Peck	Capt. Ahab
Richard Basehart	Ishmael
Leo Genn	Starbuck
Harry Andrews	Stubb
Bernard Miles	Manxman
Orson Welles	Father Mapple
Mervyn Johns	Peleg
Noel Purcell	Carpenter
Friedrich Ledebur	Queequeg
James Robertson Justice	Capt. Boomer
Edric Connor	Daggoo
Seamus Kelly	Flask
Philip Stainton	Bildad
Joseph Tomelty	Peter Coffin
Royal Dano	Elijah
Francis de Wolff	Capt. Gardiner
Tamba Alleney	Pip
Ted Howard	Blacksmith
Tom Clegg	Tashtego
Iris Tree	Lady with Bibles

Produced by John Huston and Vaughan N. Dean
Directed by John Huston
Written by John Huston and Ray Bradbury
Based on the novel by Herman Melville

and his crew, none of whom will prosper unless the good ship *Pequod* returns safely home with its hold full of oil. In the end, of course, Ahab fails to achieve his own goals and leads his crew and his masters' business to ruin.

There have been two fine versions of this movie: the cinematically flawed, but brilliantly written, 1956 classic in which Gregory Peck plays Ahab; and a more recent made-for-TV version with Patrick Stewart at the helm. Neither version begins to tap the depths of Herman Melville's novel, but both touch on the major managerial themes underlying the disastrous voyage of the *Pequod*.

While we'll focus primarily on the leadership questions raised by the film, you'll also find some thoughts on hiring, compensation, motivation and team building.

First, let's cover the plot:

A restless and adventurous New Englander, Ishmael, decides to test his sea legs and journeys to New Bedford, Massachusetts, to try his luck at whaling. He's hired as an entry-level seaman by Bildad and Peleg, owners of the good ship *Pequod*, a whaler under the command of veteran Captain Ahab. The ship's motley and international crew consists of veterans and novices, including New Englanders; Native Americans; a reformed cannibal from the South Seas; and a young, free-black cabin boy. As the crew sets sail, their fate is foreshadowed by a prophetic warning of doom from a seaman named Elijah and by a sermon based on the fate of Jonah, the Biblical prophet who questioned a command from God.

Once at sea, we learn that Captain Ahab has a personal mission. He wants to kill Moby Dick, a gargantuan white whale that snapped off Ahab's leg on a previous voyage. His injury has created an obsessive desire for vengeance in the captain's mind.

Ahab has three key lieutenants. Starbuck, the first mate,

is a thoughtful and honest adviser who is not reluctant to question the captain's judgment and his increasingly bizarre behavior. Stubb, the second mate, is an easy-going veteran, prone to take events as they come and unlikely ever to rock the boat by questioning the captain's orders. Flask, the third mate, is taciturn, somewhat slow-witted and sea-dog loyal. For him the captain's word is the *only* law. Ishmael, the novice seaman, serves as observer and recorder of the voyage.

As the voyage progresses, Ahab becomes increasingly obsessed with the hunt for Moby Dick. At one point he passes up a school of whales, denying the ship's owners and crew a windfall profit. Starbuck, in particular, is concerned by the captain's obsession and confronts Ahab about the captain's lack of regard for the owners' interest. Ahab refuses to heed Starbuck's rebuke and threatens to put him in irons.

When the *Pequod* finally encounters the elusive Moby Dick, an epic hunt begins. In the end, the whale triumphs, sinking the whaler and destroying all hands except Ishmael, who survives by floating on a coffin until he is rescued by a passing ship.

Moby Dick is a whale of a tale about the consequences—mission be damned!—of throwing the rules overboard.

Let's look at some of the movie's key lessons:

#1 KEEP FOCUSED ON YOUR MISSION

The mission of a whaling captain was clear and simple: hunt whales, kill them, process them for oil and return home as quickly as possible with a hold full of oil. When the mission was achieved, the owners were properly

> ## EIGHT LEADERSHIP LESSONS
> ## FROM MOBY DICK
>
> - Keep focused on your mission
> - Cultivate and listen to your Starbucks
> - Have a mission statement people can march to
> - Be a good steward of company resources
> - Inertia of belief perpetuates bad leadership
> - Bad leaders often have many good traits
> - Give reasons–explain yourself!
> - Look for competence, not conformity

rewarded with profit for the risks they had incurred in outfitting and manning their ship. The crew (and captain) were rewarded with agreed-upon shares of the profits. The more oil they found and the faster they found it, the greater the rewards for all.

Ahab, of course, abandons the mission from the start and he does so intentionally. Sometimes this happens in real business, too. In real business, managers may consciously choose to abandon corporate mission for reasons of self-gain, personal glory, the exercise of power over individuals, or for perceived "higher purposes." (Imagine a whaler who wanted to save whales, not slaughter them, and so worked to impede whaling operations!) More often, in real business, mission is lost step-by-step to distraction and convenience. For example, you may know your mission is to maximize calls on a difficult customer; but it's easier to make calls on a delightful but less-productive customer, so you do that instead. Or you may know that you need to lead by example and demonstrate your dedication to your company, but it's so easy to take that extra half-hour at lunch, do crosswords at your desk and ease out the door a few minutes early. Regardless of the motives and methods that undermine achievement of the corporate mission, the root cause is usually ego—putting personal goals ahead of the collective welfare of the company's owners, employees and customers.

Don't do that if you value yourself—and your paycheck!

#2 CULTIVATE AND LISTEN TO YOUR STARBUCKS

Throughout *Moby Dick*, the struggle between Ahab and Starbuck is far more interesting, from a business perspective, than is the struggle between Ahab and the whale. Starbuck represents the voices of reason, the owners and corporate responsibility. Unless you want to be like Ahab (we hope not!), you need Starbucks around you to raise thoughtful questions about your actions. You may, of course, be able to argue your way to any point on the moral compass, but a Starbuck will help you keep your direction true.

#3 HAVE A MISSION STATEMENT
PEOPLE CAN MARCH TO

Almost all companies nowadays have "mission statements." Most of them talk about what a company does, for example: "Acme will be the world's No. 1 maker of widgets and widget-based products . . . " A good mission statement is like a good tune: everyone can sing, hum or whistle it—and they like it so much that they do so.

Unfortunately, the *Pequod* doesn't have such a mission statement—or if it does, it hasn't been played often enough for the employees to pick up its tune. Ahab may know the tune, but he doesn't want it played—he has a mission of his own. Only Starbuck shows a clear understanding of the ship's mission, the captain's role and his own job. For Starbuck, the role of the firm and its employees goes beyond the mere search for profit. Starbuck is a thoughtful man who knows that his company exists to provide a needed service to the society that allows it to do business. Here's how he sums it up in a conversation with Flask and Stubb:

> . . . It is our task in life to kill whales and furnish up their oil for the lamps of the world. If we perform that task well and faithfully, we do a service to mankind that pleases Almighty God. Ahab would deny all that. . . . He has taken us from the rich harvest we were reaping to satisfy his lust for revenge. He is twisting that which is holy into something dark and purposeless . . .

How many of your managers understand that the company's mission goes beyond the mere making of profit? How often have you articulated corporate mission in terms of the larger need society has for your services?

One company whose CEO does an excellent job of explaining its mission is Price/Costco, the giant discount and wholesale club. When the Costco part of the company was started in the 1980s, its founders set out to turn retailing on its ear. The company's president, Jim Sinegal, tells audiences that Costco looked at every aspect of traditional marketing for consumer goods and considered alternatives. If traditional retailers advertised, Costco would not; if traditional retailers offered several lines of commodity products such as orange juice, Costco would not; if traditional stores spent lots on décor, Costco would not. Another difference: you will always find frozen orange juice at Costco, but it won't always be the same brand. Sinegal explains that Costco's mission is not just to sell goods, but to sell them in ways that save Costco members money. That enables members to be better off, have more control over their money and achieve a higher general standard of living. Sinegal positions consumer well-being as the ultimate goal of the company. Now that's a mission! It says, in effect, "We aren't just selling goods; we are creating wealth for consumers, who in turn will be able to save more, which will spur investment, which will grow jobs, which will create a more prosperous America!" Costco employees will tell you this time and again. Their words may vary, but the underlying theme is the same: by working to keep prices low, Costco helps everyone live a little better and makes the world a better place!

One of the distinguishing characteristics of companies like Costco is that their employees—from CEO to the newest clerk—articulate and apply their mission statement with passion.

When Starbuck speaks of the *Pequod*'s mission, he literally puts it in terms of "God's work." If the mission is not properly carried out, widows and orphans will suffer; homes will go without light; and God's bounty will be squandered (the prevailing Judeo-Christian view in 1830 was that all animals, whales included, were placed on earth to be of use to humankind). Starbuck considers the squandering of that bounty not only poor business but also "blasphemous and evil."

Starbuck tries to convey a Costco-type philosophy to Ahab and later to Stubb and Flask. Unfortunately for Bildad and Peleg, Starbuck seems to be the only employee who understands and can explain the nuances of the corporate mission. At Costco, all employees can do it!

A Whaler's Compensation:
The *Pequod's* Pay Plan

A whaler's pay depended entirely on the success of the voyage. Usually men signed on for a voyage of up to three years, at the end of which they would be paid a share, or lay, of the profits. The value of the lay was based on the importance of the job each whaler held and was negotiable based on both the "job description" and the experience of the seaman. In *Moby Dick*, for example, we learn that Captain Ahab will earn 10 percent of the voyage's proceeds (which is, by the way, a very generous share—few captains were paid so well); as a skilled and experienced harpooner, Queequeg is offered and accepts the 60th lay, equal to 1/60 of the profits or 1.33 percent. The harpooners, collectively, will be paid about four to five percent of the profits. As a low-level hand with no experience, Ishmael will have the 777th lay—1/777th of the profits.

The typical New Bedford whaleship carried a crew of 40 to 50 and owners typically kept 60 to 70 percent of the profits, after expenses. There were many disputes, of course. First the voyage's cargo had to be sold. This consisted not only of oil, but also whale ivory and ambergris. Market prices fluctuated widely. Once the gross value of the oil had been received, the costs of outfitting the ship and provisioning the crew were deducted, along with other expenses due to loss and damage. Disputes over these matters further reduced the profits available for sharing. Owners had total control of the determination, although appeals to an owner's organization were sometimes successful.

The Whaling Museum in New Bedford, Massachusetts, provides this profile of how a ship's profits might be divided: in 1851 the ship *Benjamin Tucker* returned to home port carrying 73,707 gallons of whale oil; 5,348 gallons of valuable sperm oil; and 30,012 pounds of whalebone (or baleen). After expenses, the profit from the voyage was $45,320. Assuming the owners took 65 percent, the captain and crew divided $15,862. (At that time the dollar was worth about 13 of today's dollars, which means captain and crew would have split the equivalent of $206,076 in today's currency.)

Assuming the *Benjamin Tucker* and the *Pequod* were the same size—and the *Pequod* had returned with the same cargo and the same expenses, Ahab would have received $20,061 in today's dollars; Queequeg would have gotten about $3,435; and poor Ishmael would have gotten only $265! No wonder a gold Spanish ounce worth $208 in today's money was a strong incentive to the seamen. It was worth nearly as much as a voyage's wages. And the captain's offer to divide his share equally among the men is real money: worth about $500 per crewman, roughly twice Ishmael's likely share.

When the ship *Milton* returned to port in 1836, the captain received $5,882 (he had a lay of 1/17th— much worse than Ahab's deal); the first mate at 1/22nd earned $4,545; the harpooner received $1,333; the best paid seaman earned $800; and the worst paid received $571. However, the New Bedford museum reports, on another voyage of the *Milton*, one of its Ishmaels received only $10.10!

Keep in mind that these wages were paid for several years' work. But also remember that the shipowners provided food, shelter (such as a ship *can* provide), medical care and clothing allowances. When considering the fairness of the pay plan, a modern worker has to ask herself if—after three years of working, paying the rent, buying the groceries and outfitting herself for the job—she's been able to put away any money at all. Then, too, sailors didn't ship out immediately after returning; and in the case of officers, they were usually supporting wives and families. This meant proceeds from one voyage had to last until the next voyage was completed—a matter of years.

This all assumes that the ship returns, its hold is full and that spermaceti prices haven't plummeted while it's been away. Sometimes the harvests were poor and the prices were weak—and often enough, the ships never returned at all.

The compensation plan was risky, but ideal for those for whom it was designed:

- It offered the prospect of great riches.
- It offered security against starvation and homelessness (unless, of course, the ship sank!).
- It provided different levels of pay based on skills and experience.
- It rewarded individuals for team success.

#4 BE A GOOD STEWARD OF COMPANY RESOURCES

Ahab not only squanders the sea's bounty, but also violates his duties to the company by subverting company resources to his personal use—an abuse Starbuck calls to the attention of Stubb and Flask, citing it as a compelling reason to remove Ahab as captain. Starbuck cites the equivalent of the whaling partnership's manual of practices, which clearly states:

> . . . a captain who from private motives employs his vessel to another purpose than that intended by the owners is answerable to the charge of usurpation and his crew is morally and legally entitled to employ forceful means in wresting his command from him.

Ahab may be crazy, but crazy or not, he *is* violating a clearly stated code of practice. *Moby Dick*, the novel, makes it clear that Ahab knows he's subject to a charge of usurpation. As a result, he takes steps to disguise his true purposes from the crew. Occasionally he even allows them to slow their pursuit of Moby Dick and actually *catch and process a whale!* However, as the voyage lengthens and new evidence of Moby Dick's location comes to light, Ahab drops all pretense. One scene demonstrates this pointedly: as the *Pequod's* crew goes after a large school of whales, Ahab learns of a recent sighting of Moby Dick. He recalls the crew from the killing grounds, abandoning the slaughtered whales at sea before their oil can be harvested. What a dreadful waste! The number of whales is so large and the hunt so successful that the *Pequod's* voyage could probably have ended immediately after such a harvest. The ship would have returned to New Bedford, its hold full of oil and the crew's pockets full of money—but, no. Ahab foregoes the harvest and the welfare of his bosses and crew in his obsessive quest to take revenge on the whale that has ruined his leg. Such is his power over the crew that they let Ahab get away with it, limiting themselves to grumbling, which the Captain quickly silences by promising them his entire share from the voyage should they kill Moby Dick.

How do rascals like Ahab survive and get themselves into a position of such power? Step by step.

At first, it's easy for crewmen to believe that they might be able to kill Moby Dick as a normal part of their voyage, if they see him. Won't cost the company a thing. All in a day's work. Moby Dick's oil and blubber will boil down as good as any. Doesn't seem to be any problem with that. It's hardly usurpation to kill a particular whale as long as it doesn't get in the way of filling the hold.

To put stewardship and usurpation in a modern context, let's suppose you're on a business trip and you rent a car with unlimited mileage. You have to make a business call one morning and can't make a second call until the following morning. Having a free afternoon, you decide to do your desk work in the evening and drive out to visit a golf course, paying your own green fees. The company doesn't incur any costs it wouldn't otherwise have incurred (we'll assume, you paid for the extra gas). No harm, no foul.

On the other hand, let's say you decided to book your trip a day early, stay an extra day and wouldn't have needed to rent a car at all except that you wanted to play that golf course. Or that you decided to find a client you could call on so you could book your vacation in, say, Tahiti! Harm and foul!

There is one easy test of whether you're upholding your stewardship obligations: ask your owners if they have a problem with what you're doing. Imagine Ahab saying to Bildad and Peleg: "Hey, fellows, I'd be happy to command your ship, but I'm planning to do a little hunting of my own—going after the whale that ate my leg! It may take a few extra months and, you know, if Moby Dick shows up we'll have to chase him first, even if there be other whales all around us. He's dangerous, as you know—been known to sink boats and even ships proper. Okay, by you?"

Bildad and Peleg would, no doubt, have opted for another captain. Certainly, they would have weighed the risks of granting Ahab's request and perhaps would have reduced Ahab's commission. They could have opted to set specific guidelines. They might, for example, have told Ahab it was okay to go after the whale if the *Pequod* stumbled on it, but under no circumstances would he be allowed to forego the main mission of the voyage. If they were intent on having Ahab as their captain, knowing his desire to hunt Moby Dick, they might have also covered their risks by informing Starbuck, Stubb and Flask of the conditions of the voyage and giving them special authority to take over in the event the captain betrayed his duties and the agreed-upon rules of engagement.

Ahab, of course, didn't ask anyone if it was okay for him to hunt the whale. He knew he wouldn't get what he wanted if he asked. When you face conflicts between self-interest and company-interest, ask yourself if you are prepared to see if others think what you're doing is okay. If you would hesitate to ask your boss, stockholders or active owners about your planned use of their time and money, you probably shouldn't pursue your self-interested plan.

#5 INERTIA OF BELIEF PERPETUATES BAD LEADERSHIP

Ahab's sins are so obvious, we are amazed that the crew remains loyal. But Flask sums up the attitude of the crew when he says, "The captain cannot break the law; the captain is the law." That attitude, combined with Ahab's continual efforts to offer financial "spiffs" relating to Moby Dick, keeps the crew in the palm of his hand. And with the crew behind him, he has no reason to fear the questioning Starbuck. The voyage will continue toward inevitable disaster.

Theory X Aboard the *Pequod*

An excerpt from the novel *Moby Dick*:

"To accomplish his object Ahab must use tools; and of all tools used in the shadow of the moon, men are most apt to get out of order. He knew, for example, that however magnetic his ascendency in some respects was over Starbuck, yet that ascendency did not cover the complete spiritual man any more than mere corporeal superiority involves intellectual mastership; for to the purely spiritual, the intellectual but stands in a sort of corporeal relation. Starbuck's body and Starbuck's coerced will were Ahab's, so long as Ahab kept his magnet at Starbuck's brain; still he knew that for all this the chief mate, in his soul, abhorred his captain's quest, and could he, would joyfully disintegrate himself from it, or even frustrate it. It might be that a long interval would elapse ere the White Whale was seen. During that long interval Starbuck would ever be apt to fall in open relapses or rebellion against his captain's leadership, unless some ordinary, prudential, circumstantial influences were brought to bear upon him. Not only that, but the subtle insanity of Ahab respecting Moby Dick was noways more significantly manifested than in his superlative sense and shrewdness in foreseeing that, for the present, the hunt should in some way be stripped of that strange imaginative impiousness which naturally invested it; that the full terror of the voyage must be kept withdrawn into the obscure background (for few men's courage is proof against protracted meditation unrelieved by action); that when they stood their long night watches, his

officers and men must have some nearer things to think of than Moby Dick. For however eagerly and impetuously the savage crew had hailed the announcement of his quest; yet all sailors of all sorts are more or less capricious and unreliable—they live in the varying outer weather, and they inhale its fickleness—and above all things requisite that temporary interests and employments should intervene and hold them healthily suspended for the final dash."

Put another way:

Ahab is a Theory X manager who believes employees are unreliable and have to be kept busy at anything (no matter what) or they will lose interest in their jobs. Workers are incapable of staying focused on long-term goals, must be told what to do frequently and can be motivated only by money.

Ahab knows that cash is the key to long-term commitment of the crew. Oh, sure, he might be able to fire them up with temporary enthusiasm for the joy of the hunt—especially when they are far from shore where no money can be spent. As they approach the voyage's end, however, he'll face rebellion if he can't assure them a just financial reward. That's why he first offers the gold Spanish ounce; and later, as the men prepare to fight the whale, he promises them his share of the voyage's profits. In the end, as in all Theory X programs, cash is king. Here's how Ahab lays it out:

"In times of strong emotion mankind disdain all base considerations; but such times are evanescent. The permanent constitutional condition of the manufactured

> *man, thought Ahab, is sordidness . . . while for the love of it they give chase to Moby Dick, they must also have food for their more common, daily appetites. . . . I will not strip these men, thought Ahab, of all hopes of cash—aye, cash. They may scorn cash now; but let some months go by, and perspective promise of it to them, and then this same quiescent cash all at once mutinying in them, this same cash would soon cashier Ahab."*
>
> Ahab may be nuts about some things, but he's at least canny enough to know that he can't keep good people doing good work simply by substituting charisma, excitement or other intangible "feel goods" for money! (Which is something to keep in mind the next time you ponder reward systems and see another study showing that people are far more motivated by intangibles like praise. Short term, yes; but the praise will ring hollow soon enough if the tangible, spendable, bankable, investable cash is withheld.)

Flask, Stubb and the rest of the crew (Starbuck excepted) represent a powerful managerial force: inertia. Rising up is so difficult that "wait and see" is the rule of the day. Inertia is neither good or bad. It is, after all, a fundamental physical property of the universe: things in motion tend to stay in motion; things at rest, to stay at rest.

Ahab knows, and Starbuck doesn't, that moving men from their fixed positions usually takes more than one night's attempt at persuasion.

#6 BAD LEADERS OFTEN HAVE MANY GOOD TRAITS

Despite his fatal weaknesses, Ahab has several traits that are the mark of great leaders:

🎬 **Ahab sets clear goals (even if they are the wrong ones) and communicates them effectively.** Ahab's subordinates know what he wants. When the crew first meets Ahab, the captain is clear in stating the actions he expects from them.

- "What do you do when you see a whale, men?" (Sing out for him!)
- "What do you do next?" (Lower away after him!)
- "And what tune do you pull to?" (A dead whale or a stove boat!—which in whaler talk means: "We'll get our whale or die trying when it shatters our boat!")

Having run the men through their catechism of action—getting them to respond in unison to his questions, Ahab then sets out the special instructions:

- He asks the mastheaders to look for a white whale and offers a Spanish gold ounce as a reward for the first man who sights him.
- He tells the men, in no uncertain terms: "This is what you shipped for men—to chase that white whale . . . until he spits black blood and rolls dead out."

🎬 **Ahab demands commitment.** You probably can't get away with Ahab's methods at your office, but he always makes sure his troops have pledged themselves to the task. At one point, Ahab asks the men to pledge death to Moby Dick and seal the deal with a draught of grog. Then he calls forth the mates and harpooners and has them take the vow with crossed lances and drinks from the sockets of their harpoons. Later, he gets them to renew their pledges and symbolically reinforces that renewal by having the ship's harpoons tempered, not in water, but the crew's donated blood! (We hope *you've* never had a boss who literally asked you to anoint your briefcase or laptop with your own blood!) Ahab's choice of methods may be bizarre, but his demand for commitment is a master stroke of leadership. Good leaders know that if you don't ask for commitment and seek pledges to it, you aren't likely to get it.

Ahab is charismatic. He speaks with power and vision. He knows how to inspire his men and draw them, almost hypnotically, into the vision he creates. The result is summed up by Stubb: "There isn't a man aboard who wouldn't rather be kicked by him than knighted by the Queen of England."

Ahab understands motivation. When he first posts the gold coin as a reward for sighting Moby Dick, Ahab arouses the crew's interest. Later, when doubts emerge, he offers to give the sailors his share of the voyage's profits if they actually kill the whale. The second offer is designed to overcome any sense of financial loss the men may have felt when the killing field was abandoned. Ahab's share would easily surpass the total payout to the crew from a ship's belly full of oil. In effect, Ahab has now bribed the sailors to join him in abandoning the interests of the shipowners.

#7 GIVE REASONS—EXPLAIN YOURSELF!

At one point, Ahab says to Starbuck, "I do not give reasons, I give orders." In all probability you've had bosses like this and may, at times, have been tempted to follow their lead with your own subordinates. You know better, don't you? There are several reasons why people don't explain their orders, and they're all bad:

Whaling: How Industries Rise and Fall

The American whaling industry is an outstanding example of how businesses rise and fall. Although European whaling dates back to at least the 13th century, the American whaling industry dates only to about 1640. As the market for whale products increased and the population of whales close to shore decreased, ships were outfitted for longer and longer voyages—some lasting years. Ships became bigger, capable of carrying four or five whaling boats with on-deck "try-works" for extracting oil from blubber. At its peak prior to the Civil War, New Bedford was the capital of American whaling and home to more than 329 whaleships, valued at $12 million and employing 10,000 men. One-hundred additional vessels sailed from nearby towns.

The industry and the towns it supported were thriving. Demand was high not only for whale oil (used primarily for lighting), but also for spermaceti (oil from the head of the sperm whale—valued for use in cosmetics) and for ambergris (used in perfumes).

Then competition came in the form of a substitution. Petroleum was discovered in Pennsylvania in 1859. Kerosene from petroleum was far superior to whale oil for lighting—and cheaper, as well. The industry reeled and was hit again when the electric light bulb became commercially available in 1879. While kibitzers might say the industry should have cashed in its assets and bought into Standard Oil and Edison Electric, the whalemen chose to diversify into new products. If they couldn't sell oil, they could develop new uses for baleen, the substance found in the mouths of most whales instead of teeth. Baleen is made of keratin—the same material as your fingernails. It was used for making carriage springs, corset stays, fishing rods, frames for luggage and hats, horse whips, and the ribs of umbrellas. Now instead of hunting sperm whales, the fleet headed for the Arctic in search of Bowheads which produce the best and most plentiful supplies of baleen.

In the end, however, the development of plastics and other substitutes for baleen wiped out the need to use any whale product on a widespread basis. Eventually, declining usefulness for whale products and rising public concern over the fate of whales ended all U.S. whaling operations and led to an international ban on commercial whaling.

The story of whaling shows the power of technology to transform industries. It also illustrates why direct competition (getting the whales before other whalers got them) often blinds companies to the real threats that face them. While rival whaling companies fought over dwindling supplies of Leviathans, their real competition was being pumped from the ground in Pennsylvania. And the availability of petroleum distillates literally fueled the rise of the automobile industry, which further contributed to a decline in demand for those baleen horse whips.

- They haven't thought through the reasons themselves (perhaps, they are following unexplained orders from on high).
- They have something to hide.
- They are power-tripping.

- They think *you* are being difficult and questioning their authority.

There are, of course, situations in which orders should be followed immediately and questioned later. There may be cases involving issues like national security, in which reasons truly cannot be shared. In such cases, it's good to state why no reasons can be given. Also, in true emergencies, there may be no time for philosophical discussions of "why?" But even in many emergencies, you can't afford not to raise and answer questions that explain the urgency of decisions and actions. A well-known example of this involved the Air Florida crash at Washington's National Airport a few years ago. Many people died because of communication problems between pilot and co-pilot on take-off. Repeated, polite requests for the captain to reconsider his take-off order failed. The captain thought the requests were unimportant because they were stated without urgency; the co-captain was reluctant to question the captain's authority and so held back his feelings in stating his case. The result was that many people were killed, most of them drowned when the plane plunged into the icy waters of the Potomac River.

#8 LOOK FOR COMPETENCE, NOT CONFORMITY

Shipowner Bildad is concerned about Queequeg's religious beliefs. A devout Quaker himself, Bildad doesn't want any pagans aboard his vessel. That's well and good, except that Queequeg is a remarkably skillful harpooner. After Queequeg demonstrates that skill by tossing his harpoon the length of the ship and planting it, dead center, in the head of a cask, Bildad shrewdly sets philosophy aside and hires him immediately at top dollar. That's a good thing to keep in mind the next time an exceptionally skilled applicant shows up in your office wearing a turban, yarmulke, cowboy hat, nose ring or a goatee you'd rather see trimmed. What difference does it make if that applicant writes great code, shows up on time, doesn't proselytize on the job and never fails to meet a deadline? Be picky about performance, not personal matters. We live, like the New Bedford whalers, in a diverse world where talent comes in many forms.

If you enjoyed watching *Moby Dick*, you might want to spend some time with Herman Melville's novel. Melville was a great observer of all things—and many of his observations deal with business and business ethics. He knew both matters first hand. Not only had he served on a whaling vessel, but he grew up in a successful family of merchants, knew a little about farming (he owned one), and served as a bank clerk and later as a customs inspector in New York. While *Moby Dick* is his masterwork, he wrote several other novels and novellas which have substantial business, management and leadership aspects, including *Billy Budd* (also made into a great movie), *Whitejacket* and *The Confidence Man*.

DISCUSSION QUESTIONS

1. How might *Moby Dick* be different if the *Pequod* were captained by Colonel Nicholson of *The Bridge on the River Kwai*? What are the differences and similarities between Nicholson's obsession with the bridge and Ahab's with the whale?
2. Does your company's mission statement have a "because clause" explaining why you do what you do and how your business fits in the business of life?
3. Who are your company's Starbucks?

4. Can you think of an application of the *Pequod's* pay plan to a group within your company? Aside from whalers, what kind of employee might be attracted by such a plan?

5. What product lines in your company are most likely to be threatened in the way whaling was threatened by the discovery of oil and the development of the electric light? What strategies and defenses should you be developing to avoid whaling's fate?

ABOUT THE AUTHORS

Shaun O'L. Higgins is Chairman and CEO of Print Marketing Concepts, Inc., a Houston-based firm specializing in the production of television-listings magazines and advertising services for 135 newspapers from coast-to-coast. He is a past president of the International Newspaper Marketing Association and a former trustee of the Paris-based World Association of Newspapers. Higgins has addressed media, marketing and advertising audiences in 22 countries. His comments and projects have been reported in *The Wall Street Journal, New York Times, USA Today* and in major newspapers in China, Central America, South America, Germany and France. He recently collaborated with author Ronald J. Fields on the business book *Never Give a Sucker an Even Break: W.C. Fields on Management.*

A movie fan since childhood, Higgins began using movies in 1984 to train new managers at Cowles Publishing Company in Spokane, Washington.

Colleen Striegel is co-author, with Shaun Higgins and Garry Apgar, of the 1997 book *The Newspaper in Art* and her professional articles have appeared in *Ideas* and *Campaigns & Elections* magazines. As a trustee of not-for-profit and professional organizations, she has played major roles in hiring executive directors, selecting financial management advisors, and developing capital-works projects. Striegel is a former trustee of the International Newspaper Marketing Association and served on the Political Advertising Task Force of the Newspaper Association of America. She has addressed media and professional women's organizations on topics dealing with audio information services, politics, management, and creativity.

SHOW THE WORLD WHAT YOU'VE LEARNED!

Now that you've mastered
the lessons in *MOVIES FOR LEADERS: MANAGEMENT
LESSONS FROM FOUR ALL-TIME GREAT FILMS,*
why not show your credentials to the world?

Just complete the requirements for the

HOLLYWOOD MBA™

(Master of Bijou Advice)
and we'll send you a diploma!

Okay, so it's not accredited by an educational institution, but it does show you've made an investment of time and money in scoping out ways to make business better.

To get your Hollywood MBA™, simply visit the MGTTM website, **moviesforbusiness.com**™ . Then click on the Hollywood MBA™ icon. You'll be asked to pay a one-time examination fee of $10 (we accept Visa or Mastercard online). Simply answer a series of 50 to 80 multiple-choice questions based on material in this book. (Don't worry about failure—this is a learning experience so you can take the test until you pass <u>without ever having to pay additional fees.</u>)

When you do pass, we'll send you a Hollywood MBA™ diploma bearing the official MGTTM seal, certifying that you have mastered the MGTTM course in LEADERSHIP. The diploma is printed on hand-made vegetable parchment and makes a great piece of décor for your home or office. (For an additional fee, we'll even have it framed for you!)

New study guides are added to the **moviesforbusiness.com**™ website on a regular basis. These guides are available for download direct to your computer for a fee. You can also use the website to contact us, to share comments about the guides, and to cast your vote in our awards competition for the best and worst in movies about business.

You'll want to visit the *Management Goes to the Movies*™ program often, so be sure to bookmark:

moviesforbusiness.com™

"<u>REEL</u> BUSINESS LESSONS
FOR <u>REAL</u> BUSINESS PERFORMANCE"